GRANDPARENTING
GRANDCHILDREN

New knowledge and know-how for grandparenting the under 5s

DR. JANE WILLIAMS, PH.D. & DR. TESSA GRIGG, PH.D.

Illustrations by Tom Kerr

EXISLE
PUBLISHING

First published 2021

Exisle Publishing Pty Ltd
PO Box 864, Chatswood, NSW 2057, Australia
226 High Street, Dunedin, 9016, New Zealand
www.exislepublishing.com

A CiP record for this book is available from the National Library of Australia.

ISBN 978-1-925820-79-9

Designed by Mark Thacker
Illustrations by Tom Kerr
Typeset in Minion Pro 10.75 on 15pt
Printed in China

This book uses paper sourced under ISO 14001 guidelines from well-managed forests and other controlled sources.

10 9 8 7 6 5 4 3 2 1

Disclaimer
While this book is intended as a general information resource and all care has been taken in compiling the contents, neither the author nor the publisher and their distributors can be held responsible for any loss, claim or action that may arise from reliance on the information contained in this book. As each person and situation is unique, it is the responsibility of the reader to consult a qualified professional regarding their personal circumstances.

This book is dedicated to the pioneers of movement and learning, without whose work we could not know what we know and do what we do: Margaret Sassé, (1929–2009), the founder of GymbaROO-KindyROO and visionary in how early movement opportunities are essential to produce healthy brains and bodies, enabling children to be ready for learning the day they started school; Mary-Louise Sheil, (1934–2000), whose medical wisdom, willingness to 'look outside the mainstream box' and drive and determination to understand 'what children need', helped so many families in so many ways; and Brian Ringrose (1945–2017), musician extraordinaire and the 'rose' in 'Tessarose music' who worked to write, revise, record and publish over 700 songs that were 'just right' for young school-aged children and children under five attending the GymbaROO-KindyROO program.

CONTENTS

PREFACE

Welcome to the world of grandparenting! This is a book written for everyone who finds themselves, once again, caring for young children. Your commitment to your grandchild may be just a few hours a week, or it may be more, while your children juggle work commitments or other daily tasks. Whatever the timeframe, this book is about helping you do the best job you can for your grandchildren, while enjoying the time you spend with them.

Importantly, if you are considering adopting some of the suggestions in this book while grandparenting, then we highly recommend you share the book with your children and get their tick of approval. Managing that relationship is important and we all know that there is more than one opinion and approach to raising children. If you or your children are not comfortable with allowing grandchildren to jump on the bed, create adventure circuits, make loud music inside your home or for you to set some key routines and rules, for example, then you might have to put this book aside and find one you are both comfortable with, or at least agree on what is possible in this book and what is not! Whatever you decide, we hope you enjoy reading this book, that you find some points of interest and can take away new ideas and activities that help you help provide fun, caring, learning opportunities for both you and your grandchildren while they are in your care.

About Jane

As an avid reader of books and articles, I enjoy knowing a little about the author and their background, so here is a little about myself. I am a mother of three, and a grandmother to five little people (four boys and one girl and, as I write this book, all under six). With over 40 years working and researching in the field of early development, I have become very aware of the increasing number of grandparents taking the time to help look after their grandchildren. While we have all had the experience of raising our own children, I thought it might be helpful to 'top up' that knowledge with an overview of what's changed (and what hasn't) in regard to early childhood development, so grandparents feel competent and confident when looking after grandchildren.

Personally, I have worked with children and families all my adult life, beginning my journey as a paediatric nurse and gradually venturing into the world of academia. My PhD research focused on the experiences of families and children who were not identified with developmental challenges until they started school (and this told me that parent concerns should be closely listened to!). I have also worked for many years as the research and education general manager for GymbaROO-KindyROO, a parent–child educational and activity program for babies to school aged children, developing programs and educational materials and writing articles on child development for the many thousands of attending families. Of course, not all knowledge in this book is mine and I stand on the shoulders of giants, both past and present. My mother, Margaret Sassé, the founder of GymbaROO-KindyROO, was one such person. She was a pioneer, ahead of her time in many ways. If she were alive today, she would be excited to see excellent quality research now confirms what she so strongly believed and promoted: that early movement opportunities and later learning are integral to each other. There are also many other pioneers and researchers whose work we draw from in this book, and for those interested in further reading, you can find some inspiration in the endnotes for each chapter (see p. 203).

I admit to maintaining the strong bias towards the important role of early movement opportunities in later development and learning. While regular activity keeps weight at a healthy range and maintains physical fitness, active movement is the key component necessary for building the engine (the brain) that drives all-round healthy development, social and emotional wellbeing and the ability to learn well and enjoy school. But for active movement to do its job well, the brain also needs other key experiences, including secure, loving and responsive relationships, low levels of stress, a great diet, low exposure to harmful chemicals, and lots of good quality sleep. Music in combination with movement has also been found to be particularly powerful and helps build super-charged and super-responsive brains. This book overviews research into each of these areas and provides lots of ideas about making sure you can help them happen. Happy grandparenting!

About Tessa

Like Jane, I too have worked with children all my working life. However, I am a teacher, who fell in love with my first teacher Mrs Nell on my first day of school, then came home and subjected my poor brother and a few teddy bears to the wonders of teaching because I was so excited. I never wavered from my passion and although I have only taught for one year in a traditional primary school that was the basis of my training, I have taught all my life. There have been two more people who then influenced my path. The first was Prue Kernahan, who taught the sensory motor course at teacher's college, which was included in the physical education specialisation. Prue was ahead of her time, and many other lecturers thought she was way off the mark when she suggested there was a link between moving and learning. This was in the late 1970s and she had been to a course in the United States where it was the 'latest' thing. For me it seemed the most sensible thing I had heard from anyone and I was in, boots and all. On completion of my teacher training I used the movement-based principles in all of my jobs, from preschoolers through to adult students.

In the mid 1990s I took on a GymbaROO-KindyROO franchise in Christchurch, New Zealand. I was in a very happy place; I could use my movement-based teaching (full-time, whoopee) and combine it with my other love, music. Providing a wide variety of music for my classes was a challenge as I am a three-chord guitar player, and recorded music that was at the right speed with appropriate lyrics was limited. Being of pioneering heritage and having a belief that if you can't find what you need then just make it yourself, I began making music for children with musician and entertainer, Brian Ringrose. We became business partners, Tessarose was created and in our 28 years together we recorded 700 children's songs and sold over 300,000 cassettes and CDs. Sadly, Brian died in 2017, but Tessarose lives on through the wonders of technology and is now on many digital platforms such as Spotify.

The third major influence in my career path was Jane Williams, whom I met through GymbaROO-KindyROO. I was very drawn to Jane and her incredible knowledge, but also her ability to engage people. Her presentation about primitive reflexes at my first GymbaROO-KindyROO conference had all the lightbulbs flashing in my brain. Like Prue's information, this was a real game changer for me and I have gone on to complete a Masters and a PhD both focused on a primitive reflex integration program, it's ease of use and application within family life and then the classroom.

I am a mother of a (now) 20-year-old and it was fun testing the theories I knew about while finding out that Harry was not familiar with the same child development manual as I was! He seemed to follow a completely different set of rules, which necessitated some profound learning. However, I would have loved a book like this for my own mother. Often when Harry was a baby she would say, 'And what does the modern baby do about ...' I am sure it would have helped her to know the background information and new research that supported decisions I was making, but also to see that there are still some strong links to the way she parented her own children. I am very grateful to the thousands of families who have given me access to their children over the years. We can learn so much from children if we are sensitive to their needs and idiosyncrasies. They let us know when things are not right for them if we are receptive, and they teach us so much if we are willing to learn. I am watching my friends love their grandparenting role, and when they ask me about something that is puzzling them about their young grandchildren, I now have the perfect resource to help answer that question and many others they may not have been aware of. I too wish you *arohanui* (much love) and many happy grandparenting days.

Introduction:
On being a grandparent

Around the world, grandparents are increasingly taking on childcare duties while parents work full-time to pay ever increasing mortgages, costs of living and childcare costs. The Australian Bureau of Statistics reports that 30 per cent of Australian families rely on grandparents to help look after grandchildren for at least part of the working week.[1] In New Zealand and the United States, one in four children under the age of five years is cared for by grandparents.[2] And in China the percentage of grandparents caring for grandchildren varies between 34 and 70 per cent depending on region, but that's a staggering 34 to 70 million grandchildren![3] The United Kingdom scores top marks for the number of grandparents providing care for young children, with over 80 per cent doing so on a regular basis.[4] To top this off, many grandparents also have responsibilities for elderly parents as that resilient generation continues to live to a ripe old age.

Not surprisingly, grandparents approach grandparenting in different ways. There are the overcautious ones, not allowing the child to do anything for him or herself. They do everything for the child, even those things the child should be well able to do for themselves. There are submissive grandparents, where the child controls everything and tells the grandparents what to do, even as young as eighteen months! There are the over-supervisory grandparents who don't trust the child sufficiently to do anything without close supervision. There are strict ones who follow the old 'ways' that subject the child to criticism and punishment more than offering encouragement. Finally, there are those who take a more democratic approach to childrearing. Democratic grandparents enjoy a more harmonious atmosphere with their grandchild. This approach is based on love and security, and a consistent body of rules, but with a degree of flexibility that allows for a positive flow through and around these rules as required.

Becoming a part-time or occasional parent to a generation once removed has an endless number of challenges. You might find it difficult to say 'no' or set limits because you feel sorry for your grandchild's circumstances, or you feel it is okay to 'spoil them'. Children who spend little time with their parents often experience more intense emotions and these may be difficult to 'navigate'. You might feel you are not up to date on the latest child fads, making it more difficult to communicate on your grandchild's level, share their experiences or understand behaviours that often accompany these. Or you might feel that you need a bit of a 'refresher' about your grandchild's development and how best to support this. That's where this book comes in! It's not a complete guide to everything about grandparenting, but it's a starting point for grandparents who want to know more about their grandchild's developmental needs and how to meet them, whether caring for a grandchild on a regular basis, occasionally, or perhaps just wanting to know the most appropriate birthday gifts to buy.

Being an active grandparent can often be challenging and tiring, but there are many benefits in taking a role in helping to raise grandchildren, both to the child and yourself. Grandparents can provide love, stability and predictability, form a close bond and be a wonderful role model for a curious young mind. You can bring the benefits of experience and perspective to the parenting process, being able to provide expanded support and encouragement and avoid the pitfalls you may have experienced as parents. Providing care for a grandchild often helps you feel younger and more active and gives you a greater purpose for living. You can see the world in a new way, through younger eyes. You will also thrive on receiving love and companionship from your grandchild. Maybe you will see it as a chance to apply different methods of child-raising a second time around and to play an important role in helping develop all stages of growth. Or maybe you are looking forward to just being able to have fun with your grandchild, without all the restrictions of a busy work or family life. Whatever your reason, and however you go about your grandparenting, research tells us that those caring for grandchildren one or two days a week have a healthier, longer life span — but don't forget to take care of yourself, and don't overdo it! Those looking after grandchildren five days a week don't fare quite so well, so it's important to have frank conversations with your own children about what you want to do, and how much time you are happy to offer.

What is the ultimate goal of grandparenting young children?

It's probable that the thing you want more than anything is to build a loving and enjoyable relationship with your grandchildren, to be able to support them when they need it, and to be a mentor and guide who can help them feel positive about their future.

While many shy away from saying out loud that they want their children and grandchildren to be successful in life, in actual fact it's what we all want! For many years in the late 1980s to the 1990s anyone actively pursuing extracurricular activities for young children was accused of 'hothousing', being the notion that children were being pushed to learn faster and harder than was considered socially acceptable. There was a great fear that these children would 'burn out' and that such hothousing would be detrimental to them in the long run. More recently, mothers who hothouse their children have been referred to as 'tiger mums'. Fortunately, times have changed with the research pointing to the lifelong benefits that early opportunity and experience bring. Of course, there needs to be a balance between active play and rest time, as well as structured and unstructured time; but making sure children experience lots of opportunities that enable them to achieve at school and later in life is now seen as an essential, healthy goal of early childhood. This cannot be achieved without the assistance of parents and grandparents.

Ready for school?

Helping your grandchild to be ready for, and enjoy, learning at school is a key goal of this book. Children who start school developmentally ready to learn — physically, emotionally, socially and academically — will find learning easier and experience school as a fun place to be. There are several key developmental influences that build learning readiness, and these are the focus of this book. Grandparents can actively support and promote every one of them through fun games and activities. They include:

- **Sensory and movement (motor) experiences.** These form the bedrock to the healthy development of your grandchild's brain and body. During the first years of life children's brains are busy learning how to understand what information is important and how to respond to it appropriately. Every day, your young grandchild is bombarded with a mass of sounds, textures, tastes, feelings and movement experiences that they have to learn about, and this takes time and lots of practice. Children also need to have good control over their posture, balance and coordination. The more practice a child has in learning these skills, the more likely they are to be ready for learning when they start school. (Read more in Chapter 2.)

- **Security and love from key people in their life.** This provides the basis for emotional stability alongside consistency, reliability and predictability in care and routines, that help a young child navigate and learn how to manage the normal ups and downs of everyday life. Children who demonstrate appropriate social and emotional skills are more able to cope with busy, noisy classrooms, work in groups and understand and follow instructions. They are also more likely to be resilient and motivated. Children who have a high level of resilience are able to cope with the challenges of life and learning. Children who are motivated want to learn, even when the going gets tough and learning gets harder. (Read more in Chapter 3.)

- **A healthy diet and low exposure to harmful environmental chemicals.** This ensures the body and brain work optimally to make the most of the early life experiences, to develop well, think clearly and for emotional and behavioural responses to be appropriate for a child's age and stage of development. (Read more in Chapter 4.)

- **Sound sleep.** Sleep allows the brain to lay down long-term memories and rest in preparation for the next day of new learning. Being well rested is also important for healthy emotional responses. Children who sleep well are also more likely to actively engage in classroom activities and learning opportunities, as well demonstrate greater resilience and motivation. (Read more in Chapter 5.)
- **Communication and regular exposure to language and music.** These are all fundamental to the development of language skills, reading and mathematics. Children with regular exposure to reading, language, music and movement opportunities in the first five years of life are more likely to be successful in literacy, numeracy and music-related activities, along with many other school-based activities and experiences. (Read more in chapters 6 and 7.)
- **Opportunities for exploration and trial-and-error learning**. These are essential for building curiosity, inspiring creativity and driving motivation, and are important attributes that support the enjoyment and success of learning. (Read more in Chapter 8.)

No single factor operates in isolation, each having an impact on the other. All are discussed in more detail within this book, although you will find a very strong emphasis on movement in relation to all these experiences, as without the interweaving of movement experiences the brain can neither develop appropriately nor think clearly.

How well children will develop these skills depends very much on their early life experiences. This book is designed to help you understand your grandchild's development from birth to five years and to provide suggestions about how you can support their learning and development. The ideas and activities in this book are all informed by research and while the research can be complicated (you can skip these explanations if you prefer), we hope that the activities and ideas make understanding what to do at your grandchildren's various ages easy to understand and implement.

We also provide for you a comprehensive list of developmentally appropriate gifts for each age and stage of development. Knowing what to give a grandchild is often challenging, given the vast array of choices in our stores. While a 'stick and a hoop' was ample when our own parents were children, in today's world this just does not make the grade! We hope you can find something in our suggestions that suits your budget, your grandchild and even perhaps your own interest or hobbies that you feel may inspire your grandchild. One of our fathers works with wood (even at 93 years of age) and he has progressively made wooden mobiles, wooden toys (boats and aeroplanes), wooden dollhouse furniture, wooden pencil boxes and wooden 'keepsake' boxes for his ten great grandchildren as they move through each developmental age. When visiting him, the older ones love to join him in his workshop and help him hammer and glue … and Great Granddad loves it, even if it is rather messy!

Getting started

For all grandparents there are steps you can take that help develop a long and successful relationship with your children and grandchild. It is important to establish some ground rules before you start and think about what it is you want to bring to your grandchild's experience being with you. Here are some starting points, many of which are explored further in this book:

- Know what the child's parents want. Discuss and make clear what role your grandparenting should take. Respect their decisions on child rearing, as they have the ultimate responsibility. Know the boundaries and give advice only when it is asked for, but offer help in any way. Talk to the parents about their rules for their child. Consistency is important for children: they need to know the behaviour limits and the rules they need to follow. Enforce agreed positive and negative consequences for behaviour.
- Childproof your home, so that your grandchild has the freedom to explore, move and experience the world without you constantly

worrying about their safety or the safety of your possessions.

- Try to do a variety of age-appropriate activities with your grandchild to build experiences and memories, instead of showering the child with gifts.
- Allow a slower pace, giving the child time to feel the experience, reflect and express emotions without being rushed. Make sure there are quiet periods among the busy ones and for those still having a daily nap, make sure there is a comfortable and darkened place for sleep.
- Share the things you love to do with your grandchild, while at the same time being absorbed in their interests, thus learning about each other.
- Take your grandchild outdoors. If you have a big backyard, make it safe enough for your grandchild to play in and explore. Gardens are great places to build cubby houses and 'secret places'.
- Head out to the park, zoo or beach for some adventures and memories. Nature walks can provide lots of things to talk about and have been found very helpful in reducing stress and anxiety. Expand activities to games as they get older, so they learn how to be a good sport and play fairly.
- Find some unusual things to do and provide rare possibilities to build experiences and memories.
- Read to them, as almost all children love being read to. It's great for bonding. Show your grandchild there are many alternatives to TV, computer games, etc. Visit the local library and borrow books.
- Communicate. Listen to your grandchild and encourage them to open up. Tell your grandchild the family history. Share interesting and funny events about their own parents when they were young. This is a great way to weave a tapestry of shared experiences for the whole family.
- If there is more than one grandchild, carve out one-on-one time, perhaps when the younger grandchild is sleeping; don't use this time for chores, earmark it as special time for the older grandchild.

Creating a strong, loving bond with your grandchild is something you will never regret. Helping them engage in, and enjoy, lifelong learning is a special gift that grandparents can also bring to that relationship, and the good news is you don't have to wait until your grandchild is attending school to start building readiness for learning and life success. As you read this book, we hope that you will find lots of reasons to (and ideas that help you) provide your young grandchild with the kinds of activities that stimulate and build brain structures that support not only physical and emotional development, but a keen and curious mind that is motivated to explore and learn. They will then be one of an ever-decreasing number of children who are developmentally ready for school and who find learning easy and fun from the day they start. Now wouldn't that be great?

1

NEW RESEARCH IN EARLY DEVELOPMENT

How long has it been since you raised your own children? Twenty, thirty, forty years? However long, there has been an absolute explosion of research into early childhood development in that time.

In the 1980s and 1990s, pioneers were beginning to draw attention to key questions about early development. Why were children in well-developed societies not doing as well as they should? Why were literacy and numeracy skills not improving? Why the explosion in children with developmental problems such as attention deficit hyperactivity disorder (ADD or ADHD)? What was happening in their environment? What was changing that was not immediately visible? What, if anything, could we to do about it? Then, in the early 2000s a seminal publication *From Neurons to Neighbourhoods* by Professors Shonkoff and Phillips, drew widespread attention to the relationship between brain development in the early years and the long-term implications for behaviour and learning.[1] While early pioneers had been trying hard to be heard, it was this text that finally drew the attention of medical researchers and practitioners, politicians and tertiary researchers, and more recently, educational providers. There has since been a flurry of international research activity and much new knowledge.

What have we learnt most recently about early development?

This chapter lays the groundwork for all later chapters by providing an overview of what is now known about a child's developing brain and points to why the activities and ideas suggested in this book are developmentally important for later learning and life success.

Early life experiences lay the foundations for all future learning and life success

It's hard to believe that while you were raising your own children the above statement was thought ludicrous. I remember my mother, Margaret Sassé, the founder of GymbaROO-KindyROO, telling me that when speaking in the late 1980s at a conference about the link between early life movement experiences and how well children learnt at school, a school teacher stood up and said, 'We all know what you are saying is ridiculous! Early brain development has nothing to do with learning at school!'

We have certainly come a long way since then. We now know that the first five years of life are critically important for the development of the basic architecture and function of the brain, and that this lays the foundation for all later development and learning.[2] From before birth, a baby's brain development paves the way for their future level of intelligence, along with much of their personality, their health and mental stability.[3] What has been found can be summarized as follows:

- It is brain architecture that is responsible for skill development and for our lifetime productivity.
- Brain architecture does not come fully assembled in the newborn; it is built over time.
- The vast majority of brain building happens in the first three years of life. The experiences a child has greatly influence what brain connections are developed and strengthened.
- The human brain is a social brain. Thinking skills are learnt more efficiently when they occur in healthy social contexts.
- Earlier is better than later. The brain is more flexible and learns

more easily in early life. While the brain can keep learning new skills and making new connections, it is never as easy as in the first few years of life.

- Providing the right childhood experiences is the most effective means for promoting healthy brain architecture, brain chemistry and early childhood development.[4]

Genetic research has also boomed during the last twenty years, and we are now far more aware of the interaction that genes *and* experience have on shaping the developing brain. Until recently, it was thought that genes were 'fixed in concrete' and that regardless of life experiences those genes determined how a child would develop. This idea has been completely turned on its head. Nature (genes) was often thought to trump nurture (the environment), so it did not matter what experiences a child had, genes would have the final say. But we now know that, through a process called epigenesis, even if children have a genetic predisposition to certain traits, the kind of experiences they have early in life can alter the way those genes behave, or 'express themselves'.[5] This is an important finding, as no longer can 'Dad or Mum was like that' (i.e. it's an inherited trait and there is nothing we can do about it) be used as an excuse for a child being 'different' in one way or another.

Unfortunately, there is also a downside. A child with a healthy genetic potential can be negatively affected by being exposed to a less-than-optimal environment.[6] Exposure to repetitive, high-stress situations, nutritional deprivation, chemicals found in plastics and environmental toxins (such as certain drugs the child's mother may have ingested during pregnancy, artificial food chemicals, heavy pollution, or exposure to heavy metals) can cause genes to function differently, or not at all. The changes may be temporary or permanent, depending on the timing and extent of the exposure. While some of these changes may be irreversible (such as children born of mothers who have taken illicit drugs) and may in fact even be passed onto the next generation, the good news is that by changing the environment, it is possible to minimize the effect.

By providing the kind of experiences that help build brain architecture that supports learning and behaviour, children will have a greater chance of reaching their genetic potential. The environment in which a child is raised plays the key role. Children who are raised in supportive, nurturing families where they can develop positive and loving relationships, who have good nutrition, and who are provided with opportunities to stimulate their learning and memory, initially through environmental stimulation and opportunities to move, will have the best chance to develop to their full potential.

Brains need experiences and opportunities to connect

Brain-building begins at conception. The brain is the first part of the body to be 'constructed' in utero, so that by eight weeks' gestation the different areas of the brain have formed and are starting to connect. By the time your grandchild is born the basic architecture of the entire brain is in place.[7]

Brain architecture is comprised of billions of connections between individual brain cells (neurons) across different areas of the brain. Babies are born with over 100 billion neurons, of which those essential for immediate survival after birth are connected and fully operational. This includes the automatic reflex systems that enable a baby to breathe, have a beating heart, suck, blink, cry, hiccup, swallow, vomit and move. Other areas of the brain are connected but need experiences to help them strengthen, finetune and operate fully, while others need exposure to new experiences to start them 'firing and wiring' together.

The number of connected neurons increases rapidly and becomes more complex as your grandchild is exposed to a vast array of life experiences. In the first year the brain doubles in size, with new connections forming at a rate of more than 1 million per second.[8] By the time your grandchild reaches early adulthood there will be over 100 trillion connections formed, with 90 per cent in place by the time they are five years old.[9] The brain continues to undergo dynamic changes until your grandchild is in their mid-twenties, and although the rate of connectivity slows, the adult brain can grow new neurons and create new connections throughout life.

Neurons are like very tiny electrical cables transmitting electrical impulses, or messages, between each other and between the brain and the body and vice versa. Each neuron is coated in a fatty covering called myelin. This coating stops the electrical impulse from misfiring and not reaching its intended destination, just as real electrical cables are coated in plastic to affect the same outcome. Neurons connect to each other via chemical messengers (rather than being plugged in) and together with the electrical impulses, these enable lightning-fast communication.[10]

The early years are the most active period in a child's life for establishing neural connections and building the speed at which the messages can travel. At birth, neural pathways can be likened to dirt roads, linking places with the most basic of infrastructure. With exposure to life experiences, those slow, disjointed tracks gradually transform into superhighways, transmitting information accurately and at speed between the body and the brain and different parts of the brain. The human brain requires exposure to an enormous number of experiences for it to build the complex neural superhighways that enable your grandchild to eventually engage in complex thought, skilled movement, emotional control and to be socially adept.

Your grandbaby's brain is highly sensitive and responsive to stimulation of the senses (touch, hearing, vision, taste, smell, body position and balance), the sounds of language and the feeling of movement. Additionally, in the first few months of life a baby must feel loved, secure and cared for, so the optimal pathways for emotional development are put in place. This is often referred to as the 'sensitive period' of brain development.[11] Babies' brains are super-responsive to stimulation, and this enables the brain to build pathways that exert a long-lasting influence on the brain and behaviour.

Interestingly, from two years of age the brain does not just build connections, it also performs 'housekeeping', cleaning up unused brain connections in a process called 'pruning'. Pruning eliminates inactive neurons as a way of increasing efficiency of the working brain network, with up to 50 per cent of neurons present at two years pruned by ten years of age.[12] This is why children exposed to multiple languages during the first few years of life have a greater capacity to speak these languages 'like a native' compared to those who do not learn new languages until school age. The neural pathways responsible for language acquisition have 'fired and wired' through experience and are not 'pruned away'. Of course, this does not mean new languages, or skills, cannot be learnt as children get older; it's just a lot easier, and faster, for the brain to connect the existing pathways during these formative years.

There's lots of good news in regard to all of this new research. Not only is there a greater awareness that experiences in the first years of life are fundamental to lifelong learning, earning and health, but we have also learnt that the young brain is so responsive that the brain of a child born with neurological difficulties can reorganize itself so that the part that fails can be substituted with another.[13] Importantly, the brain must have the opportunities to undertake these changes. While early infancy provides parents and grandparents with windows of opportunity in which the design of the brain structure and function can be influenced, if your grandbaby missed out on some essential experiences, for whatever reason — illness, prematurity, exposure to drugs, alcohol or high levels of stress — then the brain can be influenced to change later; it's just not as easy, as neural patterns have to be changed and new ones created and this takes more time and effort. But it can be done.

Development is hierarchical

Over millions of years the human brain has been crafted and finely honed into the complex system that enables us to survive and thrive today. In response to moving into an upright position, and to increasing cultural and language complexity, improved diets and technological know-how, the brain has developed a sophisticated structure that responds to, and reflects, the environment to which it is exposed.

Importantly, development of the brain is predictable, structured and ordered from the 'bottom up', with the basic architecture of the brain constructed through an ongoing process that begins at conception and continues into adulthood.[14] To develop and function well, the higher levels of brain development depend on precise and reliable information from lower levels. This means that brain circuits that process low-level information must develop before networks that handle more sophisticated information. It is a 'step-by-step' process, although there is some overlapping. To make the greatest impact, the experiences a child has should be synchronized with their developmental stage.[15] This is important to understand as we cannot rush our little grandchildren through development.

The table opposite aligns the developmental skill levels with the brain's developmental stages and shows how skill development builds in the first five years of life. Of course, every child will develop at their own pace: some will move through the stages more quickly and others take more time. Some will move quickly through one stage and take a long time to master another. This does not matter. What matters is that they move through each stage sequentially, with each stage building on the one before it, so brain function and potential is optimized by the time school begins and more complex levels of learning are required.

Developmental stages and ages

Age (Approximate)	Critical motor skills	Developmental level
4–5 years	Reading and writing Skipping and marching Drawing a full person (fine motor control and body awareness) Following four or five sequential instructions	Thinking skills and emotional maturation build on automatic movement and understanding of what's happening to the body and how to respond
3–4 years	Complex movement patterns start to build Mature catching and throwing Hopping Holding pencil in mature grip (fine motor coordination)	Automatic movement patterns mean higher thinking skills can improve following instructions, understanding time, space and direction and build more complex speech patterns
	Eye movement control Moving eyes smoothly across the midline of the body. Two- to three-word phrases	Motor skills more complex and refined Left and right side of body can work together and independently Handedness and crossing the midline occur
2½–3 years	Speech starts to take off Preferred hand develops Balances on one leg for 5 seconds	
2–2½ years	Jumping Balances for 1–2 seconds on each leg while rocking from side to side	Movement helps develop understanding of own body, space, time, 'how do I fit?'
18–24 months	Hanging by hands Running	Balance and posture improve
12–18 months	Walking	Movement stimulates the senses
8–14 months	Climbing Creeping	
6–8 months	Crawling on tummy	The senses stimulate movement
Birth to 6 months	Rolling Head control	Automatic reflexes stimulate the senses and movement

Opportunities for sensory stimulation

Thinking, understanding and academic achievement will be harder if a child has not had the sensory stimulation that promotes movement, or the opportunity to learn and practise basic movement patterns. The opportunity to roll, crawl, creep, walk, run, bob and jump should occur before more complex motor skills such as hopping, marching and skipping are learnt. Likewise, more complex thinking and learning is hindered if there has been a lack of movement and subsequent sensory stimulation in baby and toddler years. It is these basic early learning opportunities and experiences that help a child grow and refine the brain pathways that, over time, construct complex brain maps and automatic response and 'in-built guidance systems' required for more complex learning.

How many, how strong and fast, and how effectively and efficiently messages are transported along the neuronal superhighways — and how much information the brain can interpret from these messages — affects how ready children are for the social, emotional, physical and academic challenges of school. It is not age that makes a child ready, it is a matter of brain maturation, or neurological readiness, and these develop as a result of early experiences and opportunities.

> **The whole reason we have a brain and we think is because we move.**
>
> – Professor Robert Barton, evolutionary biologist/anthropologist, Durham University

Movement and brain development

While there is a chapter on active play and motor development, this section will briefly overview the latest research to demonstrate why movement is so important to learning and why we place so much emphasis on it throughout this book.

The research into the link between movement, brain development and learning is extensive and strongly supports that how well a brain connects and functions occurs as a result of movement experiences in early life. Movement and thinking activities are interrelated in many ways. In fact, motor development in the early years of life is fundamental to the development of *all* social, emotional, cognitive and physical skills, affecting the lifelong outcomes of children.[16]

> **Although a child is born with the tissues of biological intelligence (brain), these only become useful to the child when s/he moves and acts, explores and manipulates, sees and describes, and makes use of the contents of his world. These are the foundations and building blocks for cultural intelligence.**
> – Gerald Getman, *How to Develop Your Child's Intelligence*

Dr Daniel Wolpert, a neuroscientist and robotics engineer, studies how the brain controls the body and argues that movement is the key to learning.[17] He suggests that the brain's most important job is to learn, refine and control movement. When movement opportunities are reduced, the brain's opportunity to learn and function to its potential capacity is also reduced. Movement is the essential ingredient of motor skill development *and* the development of thinking and learning skills.

Movement affects every area of the developing brain — speech, vision, hearing, our sense of touch and responses to it, postural control and coordination, emotional stability and the ability to regulate our thoughts and feelings, as well as complex thinking tasks.

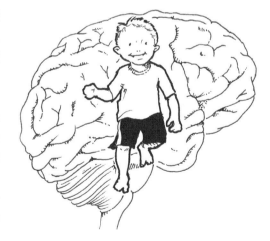

Without movement we cannot learn. Learning occurs

hand in hand with environmental stimulation, in a give-and-take manner. Something in the environment stimulates a child to respond with movement. Examples of movements that enable us to be responsive to those around us include facial expressions, sound/voice responses, or visual responses such as closing of the eyes, or opening them wider, moving slowly or fast away from something, nodding of the head, smiling, reaching out for a hug, to hold a hand or wave, and even just listening for more environmental cues. Grandbabies and young grandchildren must learn how to make these movement responses, and they do this via a movement-based feedback loop. For example, the early development of relationships, emotional bonding and attachment occur because of movement feedback loops that could be described as a 'give and take' response — you smile and chat to your grandbaby and your grandbaby responds, so you smile and chat back and the loop continues. It is through your grandbaby's movement and the feedback they receive (from the body, the environment or from others) that action, thinking, understanding, insight and planning are further developed. Your grandbaby is then motivated to attempt new motor actions, and the developmental process continues.[18]

Furthermore, this movement-based 'feedback system' is the bridge between spontaneous learning and analytical learning.[19] When we move, we stimulate both sides of the brain differently; this enables the brain to constantly update what it knows and for us to develop into a knowing being who can communicate intention to the external world.[20] Through this process the brain learns to pay attention, recognize and predict what is happening, will happen and can possibly happen and respond appropriately, starting the action process before we are even aware of it. This is the ultimate level of function that we aim for — the ability of the brain to pre-empt any action so our patterns of movement and other responses are automatic and rapidly activated. As noted by neurophysiologist Carla Hannaford:

The more closely we consider the interplay of brain and body, the more clearly one compelling theme emerges: movement is essential for learning. Movement awakens and activates many of our mental capacities. Movement integrates and anchors new information and new experience to our neural networks. Movement is vital to all actions by which we embody and express our learning, our understanding and ourselves.[21]

Babies and young children who have early movement opportunities are found to have improved coordination, concentration, memory, perception and improved confidence, communication and socialization skills.[22] These are the skills essential for the thinking-based challenges of higher levels of learning, maturation of emotional regulation and control, executive function and the development of social skills that enable children grow into adults who are productive and successful in life.[23]

Motor skills and learning

Optimal development and learning occur when the brain and body to work together in refined coordination.

This occurs as a result of early movement experiences and the subsequent development of motor skills. Motor skills reflect the brain's level of connectedness. If an infant is crawling, for example, we know that the

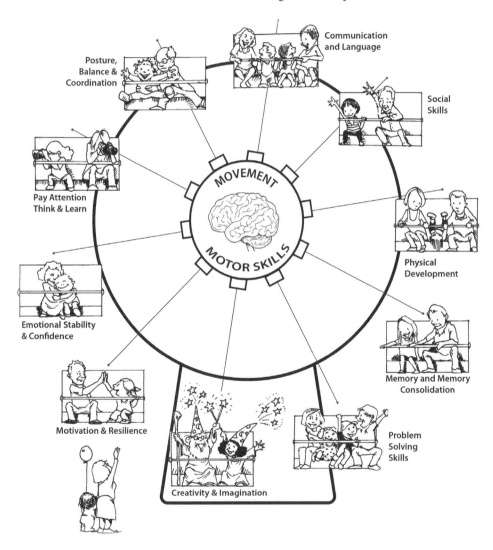

brain has reached a level of maturation whereby voluntary movement patterns have taken over from the automatic reflex movement patterns of early infancy — so there's a more mature level of function.

Movement is the cornerstone of every developmental skill. It is the axle in the wheel that drives development forward. It's movement and the subsequent development of motor skills that wires the brain for learning success — from the day a baby is born until they attend school and beyond.

Movement is essential for sensory stimulation, the ability to control emotional responses, motivation and resilience, memory consolidation, communication and language, social skills, physical development, and analytical and complex thinking. Children who experience the essential movement patterns, or motor skills, of early childhood not only achieve rewarding academic results, they also demonstrate ability in sports, social maturity, leadership qualities, creativity and problem-solving abilities.

There is no specific motor skill that leads to a specific learning ability or developmental attribute. It's the effect of the 'overall' development of motor skills that leads to learning, behavioural, physical and social skill outcomes.

We also know that children with poor motor skills find learning harder. They often struggle to 'take on board' everything that is taught in the classroom. They also tire more easily as their body and brain are working a lot harder to keep up! Fortunately, the brain is a wonderful machine that never stops being able to learn and there are many things that can be done to help. The sooner children are exposed to movement activities that focus on developmental movement experiences, the faster and easier the brain changes. My own research shows that a specifically designed exercise program that stimulates motor skill development in children who are reported to have learning challenges, brings significant long-term improvement in physical, behavioural and academic skills.[24] But even adults can help themselves improve over time as well. I know of an 82-year-old lady who started a movement exercise program designed to improve her coordination and balance, and after twelve months she was taking dance lessons and sweeping much younger partners off their feet!

INTERESTING FACT

Q: 'If motor development is an accurate way of measuring brain development and therefore learning ability, why are some children very good at field sports and not so able in the classroom?'

A: The answer relates to the difference between dynamic balance and static balance. Children who perform well in sports are more able to maintain control against gravity because they are moving rapidly. Once you ask these children to sit still and attend to a 'thinking' task, they are unable to do so as their static balance is poorly developed. Good static balance is the ultimate measure of mature motor and vestibular (balance) pathways (i.e. the ability to sit still). If you cannot sit still, then your brain is 'busy' or constantly distracted as it tries to maintain postural stability and making it harder to easily attend to thinking tasks.

The importance of repetition and practice

Motor development is not about one motor skill and one learning outcome; rather it is about the total effect that being given the opportunity to learn, practise and refine new motor skills has over time on the ability of the body and brain to work together. Children who, through opportunity and practice, progress through the motor milestones until they have mastered each one are more likely to find learning easier than children who have missed out on these key milestones. For example, a child who can skip freely, easily and automatically by the time they attend school will be far more likely to learn easily than a child of the same age who has been taught to skip. This is because the automatic brain responses are firmly in place for the skipping child but are most likely not there for the child who has to learn how to skip step by step.

Repetition and practice are therefore an essential component of motor skill development. Infants and children need many hundreds of hours to build fast, effective and efficient nerve pathways in the brain. Repeating and building on motor experiences enables the brain to develop step by step and ensures each level of development is solidly in place before the next, harder, skill is developed.

So, don't stop your grandbaby from crawling everywhere, your grand-toddler running or jumping and your grand-preschooler bike riding, skipping and hopping. They need hours and hours of practice to refine their skills and get those brain pathways firmly connected to become super-fast super-highways! Activities undertaken once a week make little difference to your grandchild's developing brain — it's the daily opportunities to practise and refine those skills that really influence brain development. For lots of movement-based activity ideas for your grandbabies, toddlers and pre-schoolers, read more in Chapter 2.

SUMMARY The developing brain requires stimulation to connect and grow. This comes in the form of movement that stimulates the sensory system and triggers a cascading effect of neural firing and wiring. Movement is the key to learning and is fundamental to everything we do. When movement opportunities are reduced, the brain's opportunity to learn and function to its potential capacity is also reduced. Movement is important from conception and, even more so, from birth when early exploratory movement patterns influence how the brain wires itself.

Ensuring babies and young children experience developmentally appropriate movement opportunities from the earliest months will have a profound influence on how well the brain connects and functions and on intelligence. Children need lots of opportunities and time to practise and refine motor skills, and yes, this involves hours and hours of active movement. Are you ready to give them the time they need?

2

ACTIVE
NOT VEGETATIVE

Movement is the key to healthy development and learning, and this chapter details why it's important to be as active as you can with your grandchild.

It will come as no surprise to you that children need to be active for good health. In fact, most governmental bodies involved in early childhood advise that children under five years of age enjoy at least three to five hours of active play every day. To be honest, that sounds exhausting, and most likely unachievable while your grandchild is in your care! It's made harder by the fact that most of today's homes are squeezed onto smaller blocks or are apartments, townhouses or units with limited active play space. The backyards we are all so familiar with from our own childhoods are fast disappearing, so we physically have to 'go somewhere' to find an outdoor space in which children are free to actively move and play.

The challenge is further exacerbated by the proliferation of hand-held screens. In developed countries, up to 98 per cent of households have at least one mobile digital device, with young children under five 'playing' on these for between one and two hours per day.[1] Even though major organizations responsible for the health of children have advised against screen access for children under two years of age, children of this age are, reportedly, increasingly addicted to screens and will not relinquish them without major behavioural meltdowns! Not only is this emotionally traumatic (for everyone), active play time is reduced dramatically as a result. It is the responsibility of adults who care for very small children to take control and reduce the potential harm to healthy development. The best way to do this is to remove, or restrict access to, all screens and get your grandchildren active!

There is an important distinction to make between active play and movement for learning in this young age group. While general physical activity and play are great for health, making sure your grandchild experiences the opportunities that enable them to develop the motor skills appropriate for each stage of development is essential for overall development, emotional control and learning in the first years of life. Most importantly, motor development is not a race. It does not matter if your grandchild is a little late achieving motor milestones. What matters is that they do. Importantly, as mentioned in Chapter 1, a young child's brain is very receptive to stimu-

lation and change. This is good news, because if your grandchild has missed important milestones, you can do something about it! For example, if your preschooler did not crawl in infancy, there are lots of crawling activities that are fun and that can help the brain 'catch up' on that missed motor pattern ... young children love being animals and creeping like a tiger in the jungle, or a cat stalking a mouse.

Why motor skill development is important

Jean Piaget, a famous developmental psychologist whose work has informed the study of infant and child development since the mid-20th century, was particularly interested in investigating how infants and children 'know' — that is, how they learn to think.[2] Importantly, he determined that moving plays a very important role in learning. The work of Esther Thelen, a developmental psychologist specializing in infant development, added further support to this theory of learning. Her extensive research found that movement experiences which stimulate motor skills lay important foundational neurological pathways on which all higher learning skills are built; in other words, *action is the basis for all learning.*[3]

Young infants think by moving their bodies. At first, the newborn baby moves as a result of involuntary, automatic, primitive reflexes. The repetition of these reflex actions helps the baby explore the world through movement, and this stimulates the development of intellectual behaviour. Piaget believed these reflex-based movements to be the basis for all future intellectual development. Babies learn by a process Piaget called 'circular reactions' — a reflex or random movement gives them an outcome, they enjoy the outcome and so try to replicate the action again and again until they achieve success. In this way, skills important for learning are constructed.

Moving and motor skill development allows the young infant and child to interact with their environment. This is how learning occurs. Not only does moving stimulate learning, but learning stimulates the next level of moving. As the brain creates more connections, it can tackle a more difficult movement task. For example, your running grandtoddler will repeatedly run up a hill. And yes, you will have to retrieve him or her from the top every time, until that learning task is accomplished successfully. Then, your running grandtoddler will repeatedly attempt to run down the hill — with lots of falling over until that more difficult skill is achieved! Once the brain pathways for the first movement are successfully wired in and become automatic, the next level of movement can be attempted and achieved.

Children who miss out on important movement experiences in infancy and early childhood, and who are not given the opportunity to catch up, may be at risk of developing later physical and intellectual difficulties at school. A panel of leading international experts from a wide range of research and learning institutions strongly supports the principle that the development and maturation of basic motor skills affects how well children learn, and that exercise boosts children's brain power and academic prowess.[4] They say that:

- Mastery of movement patterns boosts brain power and academic performance (note: *motor skills are movement patterns*).
- Physical activity and cardiorespiratory fitness are good for children's brain development and function as well as their intellect.
- In school, time taken away from lessons in favour of motor skill development and physical activity does not come at the cost of getting good grades.

How does motor skill development effect academic ability?

As your grandchild develops new motor skills, other areas of the brain are being stimulated and readied for academic learning. For example, when you have good control of your body when hopping, marching and skipping, you can balance, coordinate and time movements almost exactly. This also means you can control your pencil, sit still in your chair at school and attend to the task at hand as you are not distracted by a body that does not do what you want it to do. Children with poor balance and posture, and who lack motor skill control, find it incredibly difficult to sit still and this directly affects their ability to concentrate and follow instructions. The mind is distracted by the body as it struggles to automatically find a position of comfort and rest in a chair. They often also lack fine motor control of the hands and fingers.

Fine motor control enables children to develop the ability to write smoothly across a page. It can only develop well if the big muscles, or 'gross motor' skills, of the body are well controlled. This is because the body develops in a very specific way, from big muscles to small — from the trunk of the body to the tips of the fingers and toes. Children who have lots of opportunities to develop their big muscles through the many motor patterns of early childhood will also be able to develop fine-motor skills necessary for good handwriting and pencil control.

When children have the opportunity to build motor skills they also move the muscles of their eyes, and this in turn stimulates visual skills.[5] As they move from one place to the next, their eyes learn to adjust — up and down, from left to right and back again, smoothly and in coordination (important for reading across a page). They learn to focus from near and far, and back again (important for reading from the whiteboard and then their books/computers). The brain is also learning to interpret what is being seen. These are essential skills for learning — eyes need to move smoothly across a page to read, and the brain needs to be able to interpret what is being read. The abilities to 'visualize' (see in our mind's eye) and perceive (understand what we are seeing) are key ingredients to learning. We develop them as a result of movement experiences. Children with limited motor skills and movement opportunities often find these tasks much harder. Moving also reinforces long-term memory and recall.

Repeated movement stimulates the memory of time and space and these memories persist, so that as an infant repeatedly attempts a task the movement is refined and the infant can develop fluid, controlled and automatic movements. A baby who is learning to creep up the stairs will do this action repeatedly. Once that pattern of movement is ingrained in the neural pathways the baby will then progress to the next level by mastering the descent of the stairs. Repetitive movement patterns create an automatic sense of body position and self-control.[6]

Automatic control of movement is the ability of the brain not to have to 'think about' how to move. For those of us who have automaticity of movement, our brain has already logged, planned and plotted our movement long before we even take a step in the direction we wish to go. Adults who have suffered a brain injury will report how hard it is to learn to move again — they have to think about every step. This level of thinking and moving is really hard work; they tire quickly, and they can think of nothing else while enacting the move. Children who do not develop automatic patterns of movement (motor skills) before heading into harder learning environments, such as school, have almost exactly the same challenge, although they will not be able to verbalize like an adult who is already aware of what automatic movement patterns feel like and how they feel when they lose that ability. Parents often don't notice that a child has not developed automatic motor skills, often purely because they don't know what to look for.

The motor skill sequence of development pyramid on page 37 is designed to help make sure your grandchild is on track.

It is through movement that *all* learning takes place.

– R. Melillo and G. Leisman, *Neurodevelopmental disorders of childhood: An evolutionary perspective.*

The motor skill timeline

As mentioned in the previous chapter, motor skill development is sequential, building from the day a baby is born. Higher level development builds on lower level development and this means that higher level, more complex skills and thinking are more difficult if lower level development has been compromised.[7]

The motor skills sequence of development.

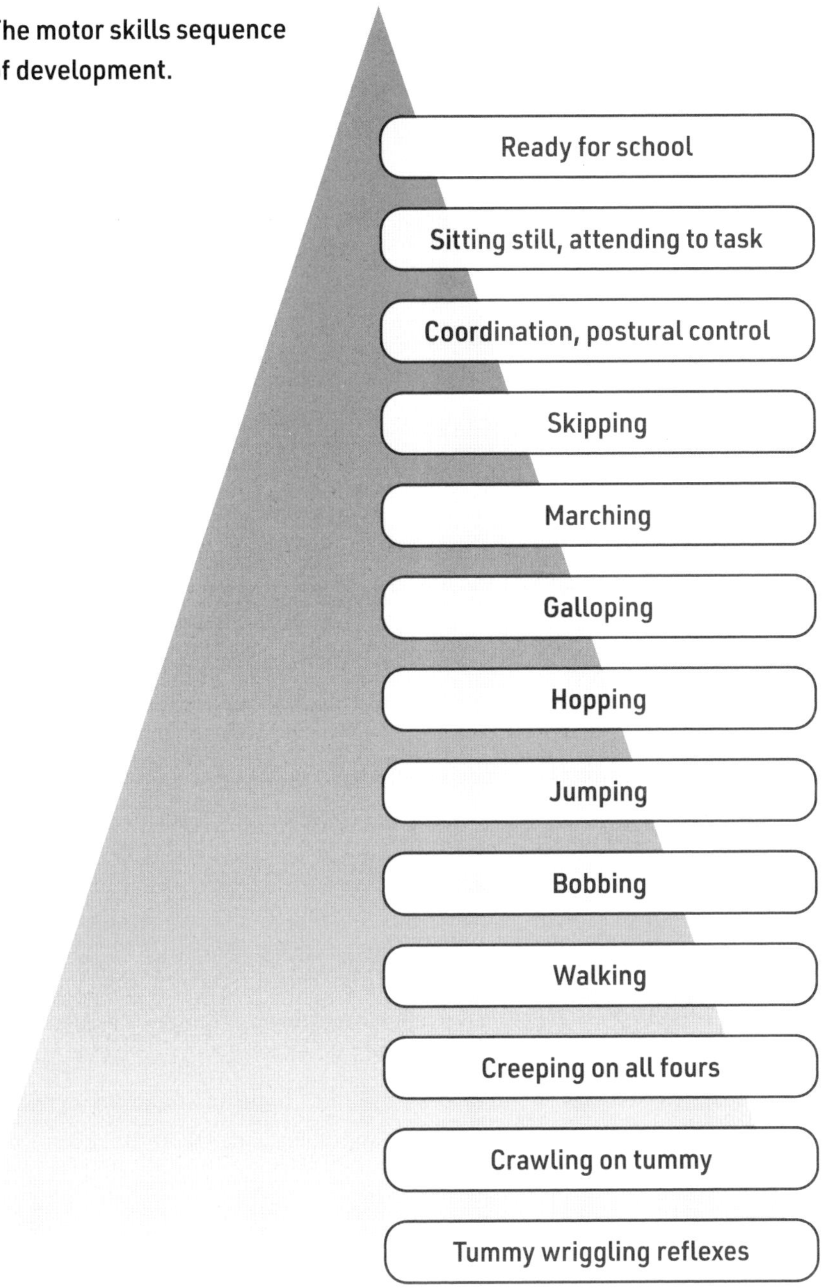

Ready for school

Sitting still, attending to task

Coordination, postural control

Skipping

Marching

Galloping

Hopping

Jumping

Bobbing

Walking

Creeping on all fours

Crawling on tummy

Tummy wriggling reflexes

The first year: primal reflexes and how babies get moving

Infants are completely reliant on parents and caregivers for their every need. To help them transition from life in the womb infants have a set of reflexes, many of which are present before birth, at birth or soon after birth. A reflex does not involve thinking; it is an involuntary action that the body does automatically. There are three major types of reflexes that play important roles in healthy development: survival, primitive and postural reflexes.

Survival reflexes are present from early in utero and are present throughout life because we cannot survive without them. They include blinking, sneezing, coughing, gagging, yawning, hiccupping, swallowing, along with many others that play a role in rhythm and operation of the body, such as heartbeat, temperature control and gut movement.

Primitive reflexes are associated with the brain stem, the oldest, most primitive part of the brain, and the part most well developed at birth.[8] When your grandchild was born, a trained health professional tested for the presence and strength of these primitive reflexes. This helped them determine the neurological health of the baby and enabled them to implement intervention strategies should they be necessary. Sometimes, a baby has a weakened reflex response due to environmental stress or trauma during pregnancy or the birth process itself. The weak activation of the primitive reflexes is an early signal of neurological immaturity and this has an up-stream effect on a child's ongoing development.[9]

Primitive reflexes differ from survival reflexes because they are activated by environmental stimulation, and once additional parts of the brain start to connect and perform their functions they are deactivated, most by the end of the first year. Primitive reflexes perform a number of essential roles: they help a baby move safely down the birth canal; they assist in survival by ensuring a baby can attract the attention of their parent; and they stimulate a baby to move without thinking about the action. The stimulation the baby receives from these rhythmical reflex movements also lays the foundation for future development and the maturing of the brain.[10] They stimulate the senses, including touch, vision, hearing and the sense of balance, as well as providing the baby with their first orientation to space, which is very different to the 'space' in the womb, and to their own self-awareness (of which they have none at birth).[11]

As the brain connects and matures enough for babies to voluntarily move during the first year, the involuntary primitive reflex responses disappear. This only occurs if the baby is provided with a suitably stimulating environment that encourages sensory and movement opportunities. Babies gain this experience through being touched, cuddled and rocked, and by being given the opportunity to continually make these reflexive movements freely, on their own.[12] Tummy time on a mat on the floor is particularly important, as it enables a baby to experience and practise movements and gain more control of themselves, gradually choosing why, how and when to move.[13] For example, a newborn infant grasps an object placed in the hand automatically and without conscious thought. As the infant experiences this involuntary movement repeatedly, the higher centres of the brain build neural connections until, in a moment that is a delight to all, the infant deliberately reaches out, opens his or her hand and picks up an object off the floor in front of them. However, letting go is another matter entirely! It takes several more weeks of practise and the associated neural wiring before the infant can release the object voluntarily.

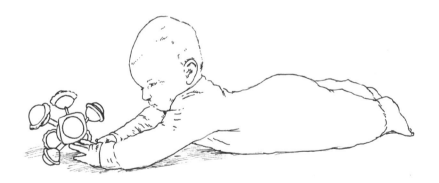

As a baby's nervous system grows and develops, primitive reflexes are gradually replaced, not only by voluntary action, but by postural reflexes. These are permanent reflexes that allow for a more sophisticated control of the body and facilitate the development of good posture, balance and smooth movement. As this is happening, the child replaces automatic movements, such as the grasping of objects placed in the palm, with the voluntary 'upstream' ability to hold a pencil correctly. This is a multistage, long-term process with grip gradually changing and maturing until a mature, adult-like pencil grip is possible at around four years of age.

A growing number of specialists hold the view that child development, behaviour and learning are based on the ability of the newborn to adequately inhibit the primitive reflexes. Only once these automatic reflexes are suppressed by voluntary movement can a child progress through the normal stages of early childhood development and develop to their full potential. If primitive reflexes remain active beyond twelve months of life, long-term development could be compromised.[14] It does not mean that a child is not intelligent, but it might mean they cannot make the most of their intelligence and natural ability, and learning can be a frustrating and stressful experience.

ACTIVE GAMES TO PLAY WITH YOUR GRANDBABY

Babies need the freedom to move. Early exploratory movements affect how the brain wires itself, assist in the process of primitive reflex inhibition and help develop voluntary movement patterns. Important activities include the following.

TUMMY TIME

When your grandbaby is awake, have a lovely, safe floor mat for tummy time play. Tummy time enables those inbuilt, initial exploratory reflex movement patterns to help the baby feel their body moving against the surface of the mat or your own body. Tummy time, un-swaddled and with hands and feet bare, stimulates:

- head control and the development of upper body strength
- hand–eye coordination, reaching and voluntary grasping
- pushing along on the floor (commando crawling), strength and control of arms and legs; crawling also stimulates core strength, coordination and the senses
- rising up onto hands and knees, rocking back and forward, and crawling on all fours
- pushing back from all fours position and sitting up by themselves. Babies who do not spend adequate time on their tummies are often propped up before they have developed adequate core strength and postural control. These babies have restricted movement opportunities and may not fully inhibit the primitive reflex responses.

MORE MOVEMENT

- Keep babies unwrapped and out of restrictive containers, like the car seat, pram or bouncer, for as much time as possible. Of course, car seats are essential when baby is in the car. Keep hands and feet uncovered as much as possible to encourage movement and so they can be stimulated by touch ... who doesn't love playing with a baby's toes?

- Move your grandbaby's limbs passively while you sing nursery rhymes or change a nappy. Dance, swing, sway, slowing spin and rock your grandbaby. All these movements help familiarize the baby's brain with all the motions experienced when they begin to move on tummy and all fours and then upright for balance.
- Massage every time you change a nappy or sit with your grandbaby on your lap – you can massage the hips, legs, feet and toes during a nappy change, and fingers, arms, shoulders and tummy or back when enjoying a cuddle. Massage helps the baby start to develop an understanding of their own body and to feel their different body parts and muscles. They have no sense of this at all when they are born.
- Avoid any screen time. Babies and children less than two years of age learn far more from moving and interacting with the world around them.
- Don't be tempted to 'finger walk' (holding your grandbaby's hands and letting them walk) once they start cruising the furniture. This stops them wanting to crawl on their hands and knees! Your grandbaby will walk for 80-plus years but will only crawl for five to six months. It's not walking that makes a difference to development, it's the movements that come before walking that really matter.

CRAWLING

Crawling on all fours in a cross-pattern format is a particularly important milestone for babies.

- It facilitates major physical and emotional advances because it allows self-initiated access to the larger world, which is linked with improvements in thinking skills such as learning about the space around them; different ways of moving through that space; seeing things from different perspectives (far away, up close); and using past memories to understand what something is, what it feels like, tastes like or sounds like, for example.[15]

- Being able to cross-pattern crawl is also indicative of inhibited primitive reflex patterns of movement and so is an important indicator of healthy neurological development.[16] One study in Great Britain that followed the lives of over 62,000 children from birth into school years and beyond found that babies whose motor milestones were excellent at nine months – in other words, they were crawling – were also more likely to be those who learnt well at school.[17]

ACTIVE EYES

The muscles of the eyes need to develop as well.

- Encourage your grandbaby to track objects – babies move their eyes to follow finger puppets, toys, people. Notice that they move their head with their eyes.
- Visual memory – play peek-a-boo, hide behind hands or behind a scarf and ask, 'Where has Nanna gone?'
- Do lots of tummy activities – look in the mirror; if you can, lie down with your grandbaby; place toys within visual distance and, if they are reaching out, place them where they can reach them to assist in the development of hand–eye coordination.
- Once your grandchild is mobile, they can watch you throw or roll a ball away from and towards them and chase after it.

Toddlers (walking to three years of age)

Once your grandbaby is upright and steady on their feet most of the infant reflexes should be inhibited and postural reflexes in place. If your grandbaby continues to crawl into the first year, don't stop them, and don't try to hurry them along by walking them! The brain is still getting everything in order and, as mentioned earlier, some motor patterns take longer than others to become accomplished and entrenched into the brain. Early walkers are not necessarily more intelligent than later walkers. The act of walking itself has not been found to be predictive of healthy neurological development, as some children who are later diagnosed with developmental challenges often walk 'within normal time frames'.[18]

Once walking, toddlers need to learn to balance, upright against gravity, and this takes a lot of time and practice. The balance receptors in the inner ear (vestibular system) are working hard to help this happen. Lots of rolling and tumbling, walking up and down slopes and lifting one foot to step up a curb or over an object on the floor without falling over, is needed. They love swings, to be gently spun and to be bounced on a trampoline, and this all helps the balance receptors mature.

Children in this age group are fully focused on moving and exploring. They dash from one thing to another, love to push and pull things along (even kitchen chairs), bang things, play chase and throw balls (even if they do land behind them). You will notice that they have a very wide-armed, wide-legged stance when they run, and the slightest unevenness in the ground or rapid turning of the head will cause them to topple over. Luckily, they don't have far to fall and that nappy pads the bottom well! But don't think they cannot be quick! You need 'eyes in the back of your head' to keep track of them! They have no sense of danger so keep track of them we must. As they practise and their balance improves, the arms come in closer to the side (or will hold onto something while they run) and the legs also come closer together. The run becomes smoother and more controlled, they can stop and start more easily and turn corners without falling over.

Two year olds have a fierce reputation for their doggedness and determination! This third year of development marks a very busy period for the brain as it reaches a stage where it is not only focusing on learning about 'me' — what can I do and how can I do it? — it is trying to sort out how one side of the body can work in unison, but differently, from the other. The genetic programming of the brain drives it to seek out the types of

experiences and opportunities that best support its development, and much of this revolves around active movement, such as running, climbing and jumping and, by the end of this year, starting to ride three-wheeled scooters and trikes. They are pretty much 'on the go' for every waking moment!

Bare feet are best

Specialists working in the area of foot development and health attest to the benefits of bare feet for all ages. Crawling, walking, running, climbing, jumping and pushing along in bare feet develops the muscles and ligaments of the foot, increases the strength of the foot's arch, improves the awareness of where we are in relation to the space around us (known as proprioception) and contributes to good posture and balance.

Bare feet play a key role in maximizing both static (standing still) and active (moving) balance in people of all ages. Dr Alain Berthoz, a neuro-physician who specializes in the study of the balance mechanisms in the brain, tells us that a child's first ability to control balance upright against gravity develops, in conjunction with the vestibular system, through the feet.[19] The toddler's wide-legged balancing act is guided by 'eyes in their feet', so when toddlers wear shoes it's like they have eye shades on. The sense of touch is dampened and the messages to the brain are diminished. This is because the sense of feeling gained through bare feet on a surface provides a relatively stable platform from which the brain can determine where the body is in relation to the ground. Once head control is fully stabilized at about eighteen to 24 months then the eyes take over from the feet and, again in combination with the balance system, feed the brain information about body position in relation to the horizon. In this way your grandchild can maintain a stable head that automatically adjusts its position in response to their posture. Bare feet in infancy and early childhood also play a very important early role in helping our youngsters learn to navigate their bodies through a space and to organize patterns of movement that are appropriate to any given situation. It even helps in the development of memory.[20]

ACTIVE GAMES FOR TODDLERS
(WALKING TO THREE YEARS)

Toddlers need lots of opportunities to develop good balance so that later motor skills have a solid foundation on which to function. This is the age that they learn to bob, jump, run and generally get their upright balance more refined.

- Go for daily walks. Encourage your grandtoddler to balance along edges, planks, stepping stones and the like, and to run up and down grassy slopes. Balance is refined through repeated movement practice, and good balance is essential for automatic control of the body. Walking after rain is particularly fun for your grandtoddler. They love stomping in, jumping in and running through puddles!

- Visit your local park as often as you can, as this offers so many movement opportunities: spinning, swinging, hanging, climbing and sliding down. Try to go during the day when older children are at kindy or school, so your grandchild is not at risk of being accidentally pushed over. Hopefully your local park has equipment that lets your grandchild move! It does not matter that the equipment never changes. Repetition and practise are important for consolidating skills. As children grow and develop motor skills, confidence and ability, the way they use the equipment changes.
- Avoid screen time as much as possible. Limit it to a maximum of 20 to 30 minutes a day. No time at all is better, but challenging to implement! Screen time is non-moving time. If you do allow your grandtoddler to watch a screen, chose an interactive show where children are encouraged to get up and dance or sing along.
- Be active inside too — build a climbing/crawling circuit from everyday household furniture. Crawl under the table, place a blanket over a row of chairs and crawl through the tunnel, climb over the lounge, jump on the bed, jump off the lounge onto cushions on the floor, etc. Make sure packing away at the end is part of the game!
- Provide as many opportunities as possible to walk, run, jump, climb and hop while barefooted. Take children's shoes off as soon as they arrive at your home — in my house we don't wear shoes at all inside ... and it saves a lot of cleaning! The line-up of shoes at the door is impressive (and rather messy) and visitors get the message as well: 'Shoes off here please!'
- Find different surfaces for your barefooted grandchild to walk on — carpet, tiles, wood, grass, cement, stones, water, sand, gravel, bricks, wet seaweed, mud, etc.
- Play stamping, jumping and running games in bare feet.

To help eye muscle movement and strength:
- Encourage hand–eye coordination activities – throwing bean-bags, hitting balloons.
- Verbalize activities – e.g. 'Can you see the red ball? Pick up the red ball please.'
- Play games where they track swinging objects or hit swinging objects. Balloons with fly swats are perfect for this! Toddlers should begin to move their eyes without moving their head.

PRESCHOOLERS

Ages three to five is the time when children consolidate the skills they have learnt in the first three years. It is the period in which their brains begin to put information together more effectively and appropriately respond to messages that come through all their senses — vision, hearing, touch, movement of muscles and joints, and balance. This prepares the brain to work at the higher level required for successful academic learning. The first three years is about getting the right message pathways set up for emotional, social and learning readiness. Movement and sensory experiences in the years from ages three to five transform these pathways into message superhighways that are required for academic success.

No matter the place, time or generation, three year olds exhibit an enthusiastic desire to play and learn about the world around them. The type of games three year olds play may differ, but all seek experiences that are not only fun, but that engage their interest, attention and, unconsciously, promote learning. Just like an infant, the brain of a three year old is genetically programmed to develop in a structured step-by-step way, and certain play opportunities support its development. This process does not change because fashions change. Modern interferences — such as increased 'sit down time' as a result of increased time spent watching TV, computers, hand-held screens and smartphones — have had a significant impact on developmental opportunities. Basic learning platforms in the brain are not anchored in place. This explains, in part, why many children struggle to learn the more complex learning skills required once they arrive at school.

Memory

Research has shown that involving children in physical movement and musical activities at an early age greatly improves the training of memory and later academic learning. Engaging children in puzzles, classification and visual reasoning, and thinking skill games has positive influences on training memory. Children with better working memories experience a better ability to focus and resist distractions. Memory is not just one of the many intellectual skills, it is one of the most important, because it directly affects every other intellectual process.

From three years old, children are more likely to remember objects linked with themselves than those linked with others. One research study found that when children between four and six years old were asked to sort pictures of shopping items into their own basket or the basket of another, they were more accurately able to remember the items they placed into their own basket. The self-reference effect occurred because items linked with the self attracted additional attention and memory support within the brain.[21] Doing something that relates to self changes how children process information. After the age of sixteen to eighteen months a child begins to recognize him or herself and 'mine!' becomes the oft heard cry. From the age of three, when a child is very self-aware, the part of the brain that enables memory storage and retrieval is even more strongly developed and engaged.

ACTIVE GAMES FOR PRESCHOOLERS
(THREE TO FIVE YEARS)

Pre-schoolers need to engage in active movement play that fine-tunes motor skill development, encourages body and space awareness, the development of hand–eye and eye–foot coordination, the ability to copy a rhythm, a sequence of sounds or pattern of activities, and to develop left- and right-side body awareness as well as the ability to cross the midline.

Encourage lots of crossing under the overhead ladder/monkey bars, running, jumping, hopping, marching, skipping, scooter and bicycle riding as well as throwing and catching. These motor skills promote the development of midline crossing, cross-pattern movements and development of a dominant side – all essential for successful academic learning.

- Parks, playgrounds and bikeways are your best friends for this age group. They are active and need to be! Their brain is demanding almost continual motor experiences – some more than others. Three-wheeled scooters, trikes and bikes (with or without training wheels depending on your grandchild's level of motor skill development and balance) are excellent at engaging activity and developing balance, coordination and space awareness.

- Inside play becomes a challenge for your preschooler – ask them to think about and help set up a circuit challenge. What can they use? How can they move through/over/under a piece of furniture in different ways? Can they set up the circuit differently? This links movement with thinking, which is essential for learning.
- Practise animal walks around the house. Animal walks are great for motor skill development, strength and using the two sides of the body in opposition to each other. They can be used to visualize (see in their mind's eye what something looks like). 'How do you think a bear, dog, rabbit, elephant, seal, duck, frog would walk? Can you show me?'
- Barefoot time is important as well. Pick up marbles with your toes … and if your grandchild can achieve that, then drop them in a small container. Fold a scarf with toes instead of fingers. Let them ride their trike, bike or scooter barefooted.

You can also play memory games:
- What's missing from the tray? Have four different items on a tray. Let your grandchild look at the items, then get them to turn their back while you remove something. They then guess which item is missing. If your grandchild finds this hard with four items, try three. If it's too easy, add more items, or take away two items instead of one.
- Pairs: played with picture cards. Have a set of four matching pairs of cards. Turn them over so the pictures face down. Take it in turns to turn over two cards. If they match you have a pair; put them to one side and choose two more cards. If they don't match, the next player has a turn. The idea is to try to remember where the matching picture card was. As your grandchild becomes more able to remember, increase the number of paired cards.
- To assist the development of long-term memories, try linking

new ideas and actions to the child's actual self. For example, self-reference effects happen when a child talks about 'my book', as it attracts additional attention and memory support within the brain, ensuring that the information about self is not lost. So self-reference can be used to help children learn more easily and swiftly: Whose book is this? Whose toy? Is that your shirt? etc.

Visual games, too, are important for this age group.
- Can they identify objects without touching them?
- Practise hand-eye coordination with eyes on the task – post beanbags into a hole cut in a cardboard box, roll balls down a chute, place pegs in a hole.
- Start attempting visual memory tasks, e.g. what's missing?
- Start visual discrimination tasks, e.g. 'Can you find a shape like this, or a colour like this?'
- Begin visual sequencing, e.g. 'Can you first jump on the toy fish, then jump on the toy rabbit?'
- Use hands and eyes together in a coordinated manner – practise throwing at a target.
- Roll eyes in expressive ways to action rhymes.
- Visual sequence – ask your grandchild to mirror your action and then copy a series of actions.
- Near/far activities – look at the picture on the far wall, then focus on the picture in the book you are reading.

This age group is ready for fine motor tasks as well. Hand and finger plays are great to practise the control of each hand, to learn left and right and to manipulate each finger individually. These are all important skills for pencil grip and pencil control. Here are a couple of examples to get you started, but there are lots online that you can download for free.

Stop says the red light
Stop says the red light (right hand make stop sign)
Go says the green (left hand wave from side to side)
Wait says the yellow light (opening and closing hands)
Winking in between. (wiggle fingers)

Car, car
Car, car, may I have a ride? (make fists, thumbs up; one thumb
  moves as if talking to other)
Yes, sir; yes, sir; step inside. (other thumb talks)
Get in the car (put one fist with thumb up onto the other fist)
Turn on the gas (move the fist and passenger forward)
Chug-away, chug-away (pretend to be holding a steering wheel)
But not too fast![22]

SUMMARY There are lots of fun activities that can be played to ensure grandbabies and grandchildren experience the kinds of movement opportunities that enhance motor skill development. Remember not to hurry your grandchild through the developmental process, as the brain needs extended time, experience and practice to wire up every new motor skill it learns. This means that your grandbaby might crawl on their hands and knees and cruise the furniture for six months before being ready for the next challenge — independent walking. Other babies may need shorter or longer. The important thing is that the brain reaches a level of development that enables it to activate the skill smoothly, efficiently and automatically. Only then will it provide the solid foundation for the next level of motor skill acquisition.

3

BEHAVIOUR: CONSISTENCY, RELIABILITY, PREDICTABILITY

Behaviour. Oh, my goodness, is this a topic and a half! Ask any parent or grandparent and you will hear that this is the 'hot topic' for children of all ages, from the littlest of babies to the most truculent of teenagers. The concerns are endless … Should I let my baby cry? How much crying is okay? What do I do about the food-fussy child, the child who lies on the floor and screams, or the one who hides away behind my legs when someone comes to visit? The questions are endless!

There are no easy answers, but whatever you do, the way unwanted behaviour is managed must be agreed by everyone who cares for the child and be predictably and consistently applied, as best as possible. There are some very helpful and insightful behaviour management books and online resources available, but before you head to them, it helps to understand why children behave the way they do and why it matters that as grandparents we need to be consistent, reliable and predictable in our responses to behaviour.

Emotional development and the brain

Emotional development, and subsequent patterns of behaviour, begin before birth and rapidly progress during the first two years of life. Key areas of brain responsible for emotional regulation are not fully matured until children are in the mid-twenties, but adult-like functional brain connections for emotional regulation start to emerge during the first year. How well these brain circuits connect and grow during the second year of life has been found to predict the IQ and emotional control of the children at four years old.[1] This means that the experiences a child has in the first years of life will determine how the emotional architecture of the child's brain is built. This then impacts how easily emotions can be controlled (regulated), how well children will think and learn and how well they will do in life.[2]

Emotional maturity, and the ability to control emotional responses, builds (or not) alongside life experiences. Self-esteem, self-control and self-confidence are very important to behaviour and relating to others, but they do not come without a lot of opportunities for brain maturation in infancy and early childhood. Rules, customs, self-sufficiency, self-discipline, self-control, listening, manners and principles of co-existence are important to emotional development and need to be instilled early if children are to successfully manage the challenges that everyday life brings.[3]

It's never too early to teach these important values and it is easier to do before a child starts school and has your support. Assuming grandchildren will learn these skills when they get to school is setting them up to fail. Children who are not prepared for the structure and rules of a classroom or school environment will struggle more than those who are. When entering the formal classroom, children need to be emotionally capable of independently taking on learning in a positive manner. This means they will be able to emotionally cope with not always 'getting something right', not always 'getting their own way' and not always 'winning'. Being able to manage emotions in this way is called 'emotional regulation' and is a necessary level of emotional maturity that enables children (and adults) to cope with the daily ups and downs of life.

Emotions illuminate the working of the brain. Emotions open the doors to learning, attention and memory which leads to the development of knowledge.

— Francesco Moya, medical specialist and neuroscientist

Many early life experiences interact to create the foundation and build emotional maturity that underpins good mental health, social connectedness and academic achievement. Young children thrive emotionally in a loving, consistent, reliable, predictable and supportive environment that encourages them to follow rules, become self-sufficient and independent, develop self-discipline and control, develop good listening, manners and, by the time they start school, how to work in a positive manner in a group without a parent guiding and supporting them. In contrast, young children who are exposed to a high-stress environments, inconsistent care and routines that lack structure and support where carers are frequently changed and inattentive will often develop behavioural challenges that potentially lead to mental health problems and isolation from important family, school and social networks.

WHAT IS EMOTIONAL REGULATION?

- Emotional regulation is the maturation of the brain to a level that allows a child (and adult) to control their emotional responses to different situations so that they are appropriate for the experience and the situation.
- Young children need to develop this ability and do so through experience, practice and the support of a caring adult who guides and mentors them.
- Emotional regulation is essential for successful academic performance in school, developing friendships and later being able to hold down a job.
- Emotional regulation enables a child to be more resilient and motivated.

Regulating behaviour, motivation, and the role genes play

It may come as no surprise that our own individual genetic profile plays a very important role in how well we manage our emotions. You have, most likely at some point, identified certain behavioural or emotional idiosyncrasies as being 'in the genes', especially when your grandchild seems to follow in the footsteps of a parent or a grandparent when it comes to a particular behavioural trait. Traits such as shyness or a 'fiery' personality are often believed to be genetic, but new research tells us there is much more to this than meets the eye.

Genes are communicators. How they communicate is determined by the kinds of experiences we have. This is because genes are sensitive to the body's production of certain chemicals (hormones) in response to certain situations. For example, a child who is excessively shy will have a higher production of a stress hormone (cortisol) in response to what is perceived by the child to be a 'scary or threatening' social situation than a child who is not shy. This elevated hormone in the body affects genetic expression, or how a gene reacts. It does this in a very special way. Each gene has an on/off 'switch' that can be described as a 'landing strip for chemical messengers', which can attach to the DNA (genetic material). The type and intensity of the chemical messenger that 'lands' determines what a gene turns on or off and this in turn establishes the long-term pattern of emotional response.[4] In this way the brain writes social experiences into biological processes. This process is called 'epigenesis' and, while complicated, it's important to be aware of, as it means we can really make a difference in the first years of life by providing the most supportive kind of environment for your grandchildren's emotional and social development. For example, a child may be born with the shyness gene (and yes, one has been found to exist), but if that child is given regular supportive and positive experiences with lots of appropriate social opportunities, the shyness element of the gene is not switched on, or not as strongly activated. Pretty amazing, really!

Unfortunately, if a child has negative early life experiences, then biochemical barriers attach to the genetic switch and prevent anything from

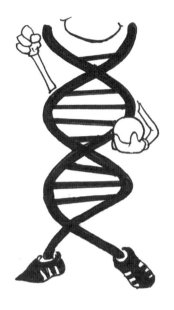

'landing' and epigenetic action cannot occur, and these psychological experiences can affect epigenetic structures for the long term.[5] Researchers have found if very young children are exposed to long-term high levels of stress then this inhibits the anti-stress gene from activating and children have great difficulty changing this pattern.[6]

This does not mean a child should be protected from experiencing any stress at all! Everyday stressors are part of life and children need to learn how to cope with them. The only way to learn is through practice. Children who are totally protected from stressful experiences in the first five years manifest many of the same behaviours as a child who has been highly stressed.[7] Often referred to as 'bubble-wrapped kids', they have high levels of anxiety, fear of failure, depression and outbursts of anger and frustration and these patterns of behaviour may continue into the teenage years and adulthood.

You may notice that your grandchild is more heavily supervised and protected from stressful situations than children were in the past. Concerns for safety have led to severe restrictions on exploration play, particularly in children older than three years. 'Helicopter parents' try to protect their children from harm by being super-cautious and are, as a result, over-protective.[8] While there is no denying that their intentions are well meaning, children from these families often end up with major behavioural and emotional problems as they are unable to cope with stress or failure. As a grandparent, you have an opportunity to strike a balance between providing security and love and allowing your grandchild to explore the world and learn on their own (appropriate for age, of course). This works to develop the emotional regulation system of the brain, motivates a child to do and learn more and builds resilience.

Exposing your grandchild to everyday stress is not a deliberate tactic — it's just a normal part of everyday life. There will often be times when it is not possible for your grandtoddler and older aged grandchild to get what they want. This is a stressful moment for your grandchild (and maybe you as well!), but how this moment is handled is important. 'Giving in' and acceding to the request/demand/impulse may reduce the tears and remonstrations immediately, but what is your grandchild learning? They are learning that if they cry, scream and throw themselves on the floor, they can manipulate people and get what they want! Of course, there will be moments when you do need to be flexible and immediately responsive, but there are times when it may be an opportunity for your grandchild to learn the applicable rules or what is acceptable behaviour. From eighteen months a toddler's brain is beginning to make the connections that enable them to learn simple rules and to start learning impulse control, although it takes time and plenty of practice!

There are some great books on managing children's behaviour (my favourites are *Best Start* by Lynn Jenkins and *Young Children's Behaviour* by Louise Porter), so this chapter does not discuss in-depth behaviour management strategies. What I would like to point to is that you can see behaviourally challenging moments as learning opportunity moments. When toddlers start to 'throw tantrums' they are actually trying to determine the boundaries in their life, and it is up to caring adults to help them learn what these are — in a supportive and loving way. Don't think that children will just 'grow out of it', because whatever action you take at that moment in time will make a big difference to your grandchild's long-term success in life. A very famous long-term study undertaken in Dunedin, New Zealand, has followed the lives of 1000 children from birth to adulthood and continues to this day. They found that if children at five years of age do not have impulse control, then at 35 years they have worse outcomes in relation to crime, drugs, stability of relationships, reduced socio-economic status as well as an increased rate of depression, addiction and poorer health.[9]

So as a grandparent caring for young children, see these stressful moments as great opportunities to help your grandchild learn to control their emotions, curb impulses and learn what is acceptable behaviour and what is not. What makes all the difference to your grandchild is how you manage this stressful moment. If you are warm and loving, and the rules are predictable and consistent, your grandchild will quickly learn to understand the boundaries, follow your rules (e.g. 'Put away your toys before you start another game'), become self-sufficient (e.g. 'Can you do this without my help?') and develop self-discipline and control (e.g. 'Almost ... don't get upset! How about trying again?'). You are also the perfect person to encourage good listening and manners.

A reminder in regard to your own emotional responses: You cannot pretend to care or pretend not to be angry or upset, frustrated or 'fed up', because infants and children are very good at 'reading' your body language. If you feel unable to manage your own emotional response at a 'difficult' moment, be aware that you will be watched closely by your grandchild! Whatever you do, your grandchild will see you and learn, 'This is how I should behave when I am angry or not coping'. The brain contains 'mirror neurons' that not only reflect and learn from what a child does, but they reflect and learn from what others around them do as well!

Motor development, emotional development, motivation and resilience

Physical activity forms an important part of the experiences that influence emotional development.[10] It has been found to stimulate the growth of brain cells in areas involved in the regulation of emotions.[11] When children actively explore, they use their bodies in different ways, often engaging in trial and error learning that helps them look for alternative ways of doing something (rather than getting upset) and after the age of two years they learn to play by the rules and socialize with others.

Active movement also promotes the release of 'feel good' hormones, called endorphins, that reduce stress.[12] High levels of stress are known to have a negative impact on brain function and subsequent emotional development, resulting in high levels of anxiety.[13] Regular active movement opportunities in both adults and children alike can help reduce stress and its long-term impacts on emotional health.

Stimulation of the vestibular system (balance organs) through movement is also important to emotional regulation and control. Studies report that people with anxiety, depression and panic disorders often also report vestibular problems, postural instability and visual–motor problems.[14] Research suggests that the link between movement, vestibular function and emotional processing occurs because there is a shared neural network between them.[15] Our relationship to gravity is our most important source of security.[16] If the child–earth relationship is not secure, then all other relationships are apt to be less optimal.[17] Vestibular stimulation through movement plays a key role in the maturation of the emotional system and the development of emotional regulation. Children need regular opportunities to hang upside down, jump, swing, roll, rock and move from side to side. Visits to the local park are the easiest way of providing the opportunities to get those balance organs active and responsive, but dancing to music and allowing your grandchild to use your furniture as a play gym is also great for the emotional brain! Think how much children love to hang upside down as they lie off the edge of a lounge or jump on a bed like a trampoline!

Motivation and resilience

Motivation inspires us to learn and to live life to the fullest. The areas of the brain that drive motivation also drive attention, learning and decision-making. These are built over time, from very early in development, so parents and grandparents caring for young children can strongly influence the development of motivation. Positive, loving, supportive relationships form the bedrock of healthy motivational system development. Young children are then motivated by active exploration, play and achieving mastery or success in games and activities.[18]

Active movement plays a very important role in the development of motivation, particularly in the early years of development when children's brains are highly receptive to experiences and the process of epigenesis can alter the course of development.[19] Through the release of 'feel good' hormones, movement and exercise stimulate the motivational system in the brain.[20] If the motivational system in the brain is not firing, stress hormones are activated and this gives rise to angst, depression and aggression.[21] Leading neurobiologist and Professor of Medicine, Joachim Bauer has found that children who do not actively move search for other ways to stimulate their motivational system. Screens, junk food and highly sugared and artificially coloured and flavoured drinks are also stimulants. They are also highly addictive. If children do not get their 'fix' they become impatient and aggressive; in fact they behave as if withdrawing from drugs of addiction.

Resilience

Resilience is the child's ability to adapt successfully to changing situations, to be able to rebound from an upsetting experience and to sustain competence under stress.[22] It enables a child to make good of what could be interpreted as a stressful situation, using the experience to help them better adapt to future experiences.[23] There are many factors that play a part in the development and maintenance of resilience. Close loving relationships, consistent and positive reward systems, mastery of motivation and the maturation of emotional regulation skills alongside cultural belief systems and traditions in many forms, are all influential.[24] Active movement experiences also play a role. Exercise has been found to have a positive effect on self-esteem, a key protective factor that sustains resilience.[25]

Laughter

You will be familiar with the phrase 'laughter is the best medicine', and we all know this to be true, but it is often not something we equate with the healthy development of our little ones, even though they may laugh up to 400 times a day! Researchers estimate that laughing 100 times is equal to a 10-minute work out on a rowing machine. Laughter also helps our

blood vessels function better and it's good for our heart and brain. Laughter boosts the levels of 'feel good' hormones (endorphins), the body's natural painkillers, and suppresses levels of stress hormones, and this makes us feel good.

Laughter is natural. Infants begin smiling during the first weeks of life. By the end of the first month, fully alert smiles appear in response to mother's voice and touch. Smiles of recognition to familiar faces and laughter at uncharacteristic sounds generally takes place by the fourth month. Laughter is also drawn out by physical activity. Most babies enjoy their bodies moving through space. The ups and downs in the nursery rhyme *The Grand Old Duke of York* or the surprise falling off Grandpa's knee when chanting *Mother and Father and Uncle Tom* elicit smiles and laughs. Games such as peek-a-boo evoke laughter by eight months.

Silly behaviour, such as pretending to eat the baby's food or making exaggerated animal sounds, produces laughter by the first birthday. This early smiling and laughing usually takes place as a response to familiar people and situations. Babies love songs that include games of anticipation, such as *Round and Round the Garden*. Bringing a favourite toy to life or using a puppet with humorous animation inspires gales of laughter. Preschoolers like to share a baby's sense of humour and enjoy being the centre of baby's attention. They can play peek-a-boo, make funny sounds and 'tickle' them quite vigorously and the baby loves it all! Older children can build a tower of blocks and allow the baby to demolish it. They can have a little conversation on the baby's toy phone.

A sense of humour begins to develop in the second year when the child loves to engage in make-believe. It is mostly connected to common play activities. Much of the laughter is a release of excitement built up through physical activity. 'Acting silly' often is a result of the child demonstrating a mastery of physical skills. Running, jumping or excited screaming are all evidence of a child's humour. My toddling grandsons all loved to play chase, laughing all the way around the house as I pretended to run after them; even though they fell over their own feet, ran into furniture, tripped on door ledges, they got up and continued running and laughing!

For three-year-olds, group exuberance is often found; a spontaneous shout of glee when one child becomes excited about catching the bubbles and others join in. A spontaneous wave of laughter can spread through a group of playing children. When playing a body-part awareness game, a three-year-old may show her sense of humour with a mischievous grin and touch her knee when you've asked her to touch her elbow. It's very humorous to her. The three-year-old laughs at books that include people or animals doing the wrong thing or people behaving badly.

Psychologists tell us that laughter helps children to make sense of their world and enjoy life. It promotes sociability, empathy, self-esteem and problem solving. Laughter breeds happiness and positive feelings and binds family members together. Setting aside special times to seek out humour and laughter through sharing rhymes and books that match children's intellectual abilities can reinforce the importance of laughter and fun.

Grandparents and parents who share their own funny experiences and generally try to see the humour in day-to-day challenges are more likely to raise children who like to laugh and can roll with life's challenges. My own father is currently in his mid-nineties and a wonderful great-grandfather to ten children. He has laughed his way through the toughest of times — the Great Depression of the 1930s, World War II, financial hardship and family loss. He constantly tells me that laughter brings people together, reduces worries and explains why he has lived so long! So it's worth taking the time to nurture and enjoy your grandchild's promising sense of humour through your own willingness to be playful and to laugh with them. Look for fun and humour in everything! Even bringing a sense of humour to discipline works and helps everyone move more positively past a challenging moment.

Is your grandchild struggling with behavioural challenges?

Problems underlying poor behaviour are not obvious to many people. Sometimes, poor behaviour is caused by developmental 'glitches' within the child's brain. It is not the fault of the parents, nor a deliberate act by the child, and we know this because poor behaviour can be found in children who have great parents and a good social environment. While people are beginning to realize that when a child has problems learning there may be something wrong with the way his or her brain is functioning, they do not always understand that behaviour problems are also brain-based.

Of course, many aspects of the environment are extremely important in determining how behaviour develops and expresses itself and environmental experiences can help ameliorate a potential behaviour-related problem. But there is a circular nature to behaviour problems, as a child's ability to interact with the environment is determined by the way his or her brain functions. Just as there are brains that cannot cope with loud noises, there are brains that cannot cope with stress, changes in plans, paying attention, sharing with others or sitting still. So while the environment is positive and may benefit many other children, a child with a developmental problem that affects behaviour might not be able to make the most of it. This does not mean there is nothing that can be done. Importantly, this child needs opportunities that help the brain function more effectively and efficiently, and this means lots of appropriate sensory and movement experiences, the right diet and care that is consistent, warm, patient and responsive.

How movement and the sensory system affect behaviour
When the functions of the brain are whole and balanced, good behaviour is a natural outcome. The brain's behavioural responses are based upon a foundation of sensory-motor processes. The senses tell the brain what is happening to the body and in the environment around. They are stimulated by movement. At birth, the brain is not all that good at interpreting these complex messages, but with practice and time the brain begins to be able to sort, understand and act appropriately in response to the messages. By the time your grandchild starts school, the brain should be able to do this without being confused and without delay.

If the sensory-motor processes are well developed in the first seven years of life, your grandchild will have an easier time learning how to behave. If the brain does a poor job of understanding the sensations, this

will interfere with learning how to behave. Grandchildren with sensory-motor integration problems are apt to give the family more trouble than other children. They are less happy and things are just not right for them. They are fussy and cannot enjoy being with the family or playing with other children, as much as normal children do. Losing a game is very threatening to their incomplete self-concept and so they ruin games. Sharing toys or food is difficult. They are forever trying to make themselves feel important, so they cannot think about the needs of others. Because their brain responds differently, they react differently to circumstances. They are overly sensitive, and their feelings are often hurt. They cannot cope with everyday situations or new and unfamiliar situations. They become very anxious as they do not always understand what is happening, nor what is expected of them. This anxiety can turn a child into a virtual firecracker, ready to explode at the slightest provocation.

Your grandchild's insecurities increase whenever they notice that other children are successful with some tasks, at which they fail. As a result, they become negative and resistive. They may be unable to keep control of their emotions and be happy one minute and crying the next, for no obvious reason. An insecure grandchild might behave like a baby to deal with their situations, as they do not have the neurological competence to act their age in dealing with things. If this is your grandchild, they need close adult support and reassurance for more years than most children. They need adults to understand that they do not see the world the same way as everyone else. But above all, this grandchild needs opportunities for sensory-motor stimulation and vestibular development through lots of appropriate movement to help their brain function more efficiently.

Behaviour and food

The food children eat can have a big impact on how well brains and bodies function, and 'poor' behaviour is often the first sign of trouble. Over the past 40 years there has been increasing evidence that shows a very important connection between the gut (what we eat) and the brain (how well we think and behave). Foods that your grandchild eats may irritate both the gut and the developing brain.[26] 'Fast food' and processed foods with sugar, preservatives, additives, flavourings (natural as well as artificial), and added chemicals of all kinds (to make it taste good or last a long time) play havoc with children's digestive systems, and this affects how well the brain works. Some foods considered 'natural' may also be irritating a child's digestive and nervous systems. Many 'natural' foods such as bread, butter, yoghurt, milk and juice contain additives that we do not expect to be there. For those who react emotionally to specific foods or chemicals, life can be very difficult.

Without the correct nutrition a child will have difficulty learning, exhibit poor behaviour, inattention and concentration. They will have low energy levels, or on the opposite end, be hyperactive. It can affect sleep, social development, and their ability to focus and understand what is expected of them. Poor behaviour is often the most visible problem, but it is also often the first noticeable change once the offending food groups or chemical additives are removed. In combination with loving, positive care and regular activity (motor stimulation), children often improve very quickly. Dietitians and nutritionists can help make sure your grandchild eats a well-balanced diet even when they are unable to eat certain foods. Some children may need to stay off the offending food groups or additives for a long time; others will be able to tolerate small amounts occasionally, such as at a party. Only time and testing will tell!

For further details on the effect of food on the developing brain, see Chapter 4, 'Guts and Brains'.

Strategies that support and build great behaviour

Developing an understanding of the stages of your grandchild's behaviour is very important. This helps you understand what is developmentally typical for their age and to be mindful of how to manage the behaviour accordingly.

Infants (birth to twelve months)

When born, your grandbaby is controlled by the primitive reflex responses. Their nervous system enables them to assess whether something is safe or unsafe and to respond accordingly. Babies are fully dependent on key caregivers. To attract attention when hungry, cold, sick or in pain, they cry. Infants need prompt response to their needs so they can feel safe and cared for. The development of strong, positive bonds with their primary carer at this age is essential for healthy emotional development. Supportive extended families and communities also play an extremely important role, particularly if the mother is unwell, has postnatal depression or is struggling with the new responsibilities.

Your older grandbaby will start to use actions to communicate likes or dislikes. For example, if infants don't like a specific food they will spit it out or turn their head away. However, if a particular food is liked, they will show excitement by waving their arms, smiling and kicking legs.

Very young infants have no understanding for consciously intentional behaviour. For example, a crawling infant will attempt to climb furniture without regard for height or safety. Your grandbaby doesn't understand that this is dangerous behaviour: he or she is just exploring. Grandbabies from six to twelve months also have no conscious understanding of how to interact with unknown others. For example, when interacting with another infant you might notice them grabbing toys from them. This is because your grandbaby is unable to understand the concept of sharing at this stage.

STRATEGIES TO SUPPORT BEHAVIOUR

- Loving, caring one-on-one relationships are essential for healthy emotional development.
- Be responsive to your young grandbaby's needs. Facial expression, tone of voice and gentleness of touch all reassure baby that they are cared for. Lots of cuddles are enjoyed by most.
- When caring for your grandbaby, establish a familiar, consistent routine. Consistency lets your grandbaby know that the world they live in is predictable. This helps give your grandbaby a sense of security.
- Play with your grandbaby — while they lie on their tummy on the floor, or on your lap or in your arms. Babies love rhyming songs, along with different kinds of movements such as rocking, jiggling, swaying, swinging. These stimulate the senses, encourage movement and are lots of fun!
- For older grandbabies, use distraction when redirecting behaviour. They are very easily distracted! For example, if your grandbaby likes to pull your hair or take your glasses off your face, stop them by gently holding their hands and redirect attention to another object with which they can play.

Toddlers (twelve to 24 months)

Your grandtoddler is beginning to explore cause-and-effect relationships — for example, when you are hungry, you eat. But they still cannot consciously plan actions or have control over them. They do not have the capacity to understand, remember or obey rules except those that are very simple. While they become interested in other children, having to share is developmentally incompatible at this stage. They are still learning about themselves. They are beginning to develop independence, and this means they might start to test boundaries.

STRATEGIES TO SUPPORT BEHAVIOUR

- Provide consistent rules and routines. Remember it takes time for your grandtoddler to learn these, so consistency is of the essence.
- Distract where possible. Toddlers have concentration periods of a few seconds, so that makes it easy to distract them.
- Avoid using the words 'no' and 'don't' all the time. Look for what is 'right' in what they are doing (hard sometimes) and comment on that.
- Provide positive encouragement. Praise when they achieve a new skill.
- Ignore minor misbehaviours.
- This age loves 'helping' with household chores! If you are cleaning, provide them with a cloth or a broom and let them clean as well! Give lots of praise and thanks for their 'help'.
- Let your grandtoddler be active. Their brain is extremely responsive to movement and this is how they are learning and developing emotional regulation. If you have a small or no backyard try to go to the local park where they are free to run, climb and swing as much as their brains and bodies demand.
- If your grandtoddler is with you regularly, put in place a simple sleep-time routine. For a daytime nap perhaps a story can be read after the nappy change and before bed. In the evening this could include a bath, story, teeth-brushing and saying goodnight to all.

Two to three years

Two year olds are incredibly inquisitive and have a drive to be more independent, to move and explore, and to find their own limits. They want to do everything by themselves. They become easily frustrated when things don't turn out as expected. They often begin to test the limits of behaviour and can throw tantrums that seem way out of proportion to the problem! Everything they have is 'mine!', so sharing is still hard, as is waiting, turn-taking and impulse control.

Closer to three years of age, they start to establish friendships and enjoy the company of other children. They want to please adults and will follow simple rules to do so. They are beginning to comprehend the relationship between actions and consequences.

STRATEGIES TO SUPPORT BEHAVIOUR

- Encourage exploration. They learn by doing and need lots of time for active play. You will see them attempt to discover different ways of 'playing'. They will empty every container or box they can reach and pull books off the shelf. They will knock over a big sister's tower of blocks by 'bulldozing' straight through it and they will pull apart puzzles, tear paper and basically 'destroy' whatever is destructible! This is how they learn. Use baby gates, lock cupboards and put away breakables – so anything your grandtoddler can reach can be acceptably considered 'fair game'! This means you are not always saying 'no' and your grandtoddler is learning through exploration.
- Set boundaries. Even this young age group needs to learn what is acceptable behaviour and what is not. Keep rules simple and apply them consistently.
- Look for ways to make your grandtoddler laugh. Do silly things, play silly games. They love being chased! Clear a running pathway in your house so it's safe.
- Don't rush your grandtoddler. While they are constantly on the move, they are not good at being 'hurried' and this may precipitate a 'meltdown'. Give yourself and your grandtoddler plenty of time to get ready for outings etc.
- Put in place a consistent sleep routine and regular time for bed. If your grandtoddler is only visiting, try to provide the same sleeping environment (room, bed/cot) each time.

Three to five years

Three-year-olds are full of the joy of life and wonder. They are much more 'in control' of their own emotions, although they can still have 'their moments' and when conflict arises with their peers or siblings they will still seek your assistance. They can swing from happy, independent beings one moment to wanting to be babied the next. The rapid development of speech means that they can express their emotions verbally, so there tends to be an increase in spoken expression and a decrease in the behavioural component to emotional challenges. This is such a social age and one in which emotions are still up and down. Emotional regulation skills start to mature with practice, guidance and support.

STRATEGIES TO SUPPORT BEHAVIOUR

This age group needs to:
- have the opportunity to explore independently, balanced with a consistent set of rules and routines
- experience positive reassurance and the opportunity to learn through 'trial and error' (not always getting something 'right')
- develop an understanding of, and respect for, rules
- be shown how to behave and react through your own behaviour and reactions
- talk about feelings: 'Do you feel upset/angry/sad?' Talk about what you can do to change how you feel
- laugh together. Children of this age love silly songs, rhymes and jokes
- hear words that are positive and supportive: 'You are great at drying the dishes, thank you!'; 'I like the way you made your bed and tidied up your room'; 'You are so kind to your brother'; 'Thank you for sharing your toys; that was very generous of you', 'You are a good listener' etc.
- learn about time and when activities must end. For example, 'You may have three more minutes of play, and then it is

bath-time.' This helps prevent tantrums when time for play is finished. It can also be successfully used to end a period of screen time: 'You have just five more minutes of TV.' Be consistent and if you say 5 minutes then it must be 5 minutes and the TV must go off! Using a timer helps everyone

- be given the feeling they have a positive future and to feel positive about that: 'You are so good at reading your books, you are going to love school!'; 'You are so helpful, the teacher will be pleased to have you in her classroom'; 'When you grow up, you will do very well at whatever you want to be'

- a consistent goodnight routine and regular time for bed that enables your grandchild to have a good night's sleep.

SUMMARY Behaviour and behaviour management is always going to be challenging as very young grandchildren are learning how to control their emotions and behaviours from scratch. Guiding, managing and helping children learn self-control and self-regulation is the responsibility of the adults who look after them. If you are regularly caring for a grandchild or grandchildren, make sure you take the time to sit down with your own children and agree on how 'challenging moments' will be managed. Importantly, everyone needs to stick to the agreed-upon strategy as best as they can. Consistency, reliability and predictability are the key to healthy, long-term emotional stability and mental health.

4

GUTS AND BRAINS (OR, NO JUNK FOOD AT NANNA'S)

I have little doubt that you are aware of the importance of your grand-child eating nutritionally valuable food and perhaps you are even tempted to 'skip' this chapter as you feel confident in your knowledge and ability to provide them with the healthiest of foods. Perhaps you're even making and baking everything at home yourself! You are likely to be aware that 'junk food' provides less-than-optimal nutrition, that sugar should be avoided, especially in carbonated drinks, and that your grandchild should eat fresh fruit and vegetables alongside a balanced intake of carbohydrates and meats. So how can I convince you it's worth reading further? Perhaps I should ask you a few questions. Do you know that your grandchild's gut can affect their brain, learning and behaviour? Do you know guts can 'leak'? Are you aware that children today are far more likely to develop food allergies and intolerances than children of the past? Or that the foods they may be intolerant to are often the 'healthy, fresh' foods recommended on the 'healthy food pyramid'? No? Then read further!

We shall start with the link between guts and brains.

Guts and brains

You might think this an odd pairing, but how well children think and behave is not only linked to what they eat but may also be directly linked to how well their gut is working in relation to its capacity to absorb and direct essential nutrients to the body and brain.[1] Research over the past 20 years has pointed more and more to the direct effect the gut has on the brain.

The human gastro-intestinal tract is often more simply referred to as 'the gut'. It is basically a very long tube that runs between the mouth and the anus. Its key role is to transport food, mush it up, break it down and absorb the nutrients the body requires, before expelling any indigestible leftovers.

The gut grows rapidly in the last fifteen weeks of gestation and continues to grow until the late teenage years. At birth, it is ready to digest and absorb nutrients from the mother's milk. However, until birth it has been 'housed' in a sterile environment, and to be able to digest more complex foods it needs the help of bacteria. Exposure to bacteria through the birth process and the environment over the next two years rapidly increases bacteria in the gut. By the time the gut is mature it will carry over 1500 different species of bacteria. In fact, humans have ten times more bacteria in their gut than the rest of the body.[2]

The gut bacteria plays a very important role. Not only does it break down food for digestion, but it produces vitamins K and B, helps develop the immune system, and helps protect the body from the invasion of dangerous pathogens through antibacterial properties and by developing a protective coating on the gut wall. Serotonin, the 'feel good' hormone responsible for our mood/happiness, and dopamine, responsible for motivation, are also produced in the gut then transported to the brain.[3]

The kind of bacteria your grandbaby has in their gut will depend on how they were born and what they were fed after birth. Naturally born babies have bacteria similar to their mother's birth canal. Babies born by caesarean section have gut bacteria similar to their mother's skin. Interestingly, all babies who are breastfed have been found to have the same gut bacteria as their mother, no matter where they live and what diet their mother eats. Breastmilk has a major influence on gut flora, providing microbes and also feeding microbes, so when a baby is weaned the gut flora is close to adult form. Bottle-fed babies develop a completely different gut flora to breastfed babies and even to that of their parents. Once a baby is weaned onto solid foods the gut bacteria begins to show regional (or even localized) variation and to be similar to that of their parents.[4]

Young children and adults can have their gut bacteria altered by lifestyle factors such as exercise, cigarette smoke, alcohol and pollution, and chronic inflammation caused by eating foods that create gut irritation or allergic responses. Sickness and high levels of stress have also been found to affect gut bacteria. Treating illnesses with antibiotics not only kills the bacteria making us sick, it also wipes out much of the gut bacteria needed for digestion and healthy gut function. A recovery period after exposure to antibiotics can last two weeks to two months This provides an opportunity for other microbes or pathogens to overgrow. Antibiotics are also often found in the foods we eat, and so we are constantly undermining our gut bacteria and health.[5]

Gut flora is also getting worse from generation to generation because gut flora is passed from grandmother to daughter to baby.[6] Over the generations there has been an increase in the intake of antibiotics, junk food, chemicals and toxins that affect gut flora. Children's guts are not working as well as they used to due to:
- antibiotics in everything we eat
- antibiotics given to mothers during or after birth

- an increase in bottle feeding
- additives and preservatives in all processed food
- an increased amount of processed food in the daily diet
- generations of poor guts as a result of antibiotics, junk food, chemicals and toxins
- chemicals in the environment — especially those found in plastics that leak when heated or microwaved
- being 'too clean', which is detrimental to gut bacteria numbers and children's immune system development.

This means our youngest generation is likely to have more gut and immune system problems and more 'intolerances' and allergies to food as the gut is not as exposed to, nor as 'populated' with, bacteria as it should be. Babies born by caesarean section have also been found to be are far more likely to develop food allergies than babies born via the birth canal.[7]

Children diagnosed with autism and autism spectrum disorders (ASD) have been found to have lower numbers and diversity of gut bacteria. Interestingly, they do not have certain types of bacteria seen in other children. Whether this is a function of the environment in which they live, or whether the disorder affects how the gut functions has not been clearly determined. What has been observed is that children with worse gut function have an increased severity of the disorder. They have poorer attention and more behavioural challenges. In other words, how well a gut works may affect how well the brain works too.[8] Gut function could also be linked to the development of the brain in young children, a concern currently under active investigation.

What we do know is that the environment babies and small children are exposed to will affect gut function. Children who have poor nutrition and gut health may have difficulty learning, exhibit poor behaviour, be sluggish and have limited energy, or on the opposite end, be hyperactive.[9] They may struggle with obesity, or else be malnourished and fail to thrive, or be prone to infections, reducing the likelihood of regularly participating in active movement, further depriving the brain of essential experiences

of development. Poor nutrition and gut health can affect a child's sleep patterns, their social development, and their ability to focus and understand what's expected of them. They may have symptoms that mimic or exacerbate those of children with specific developmental disorders such as ADHD, OCD and those on the autistic spectrum.[10]

The 'leaky gut'

Sometimes guts are so damaged that the gut wall, which normally forms a barrier to the rest of the body, controlling what gets through to the bloodstream, becomes 'leaky' and food, toxins and bugs that should not pass through, do.[11] These substances are regarded as 'foreign' to the body's defence system and so the body produces antibodies against what were once harmless and innocuous foods. This is how food allergies are created.

These foreign foods can sometimes cross the blood–brain barrier and irritate the developing brain. Behavioural problems such as poor sleep, tantrums and aggression are often the first and most obvious sign that a child might have a 'leaky gut'.[12]

Foods that could cause gut-brain issues

When a child has a poorly functioning gut, the body becomes unable to tolerate what would normally be considered healthy foods. Food intolerances are not allergies; rather they are a reaction to a natural chemical in the food, or an artificial chemical added to the food. While they can affect children's behaviour and development, they are not as serious as allergies. Allergies are an immune system reaction to certain foods which, when severe, need medical monitoring and intervention. The information in the rest of this chapter refers to food intolerances. If your grandchild has allergies, then it is likely they are already in the care of medical professionals.

Environmental chemicals, gut and brain health

Your grandchild's gut and brain are not only affected by the food they eat but also by the chemicals they ingest and which abound in the environment in which they live. Most of us are already very familiar with the effect of certain environmental chemicals on brains and bodies, such as PVC in teething rings and toys, asbestos and lead paint, now banned in most countries. Unfortunately, the list of hazardous chemicals is not limited to these few.

Dr Walter Lichtenstieger, neuroscientist and endocrinologist from the University of Zurich, reports that our grandchildren's exposure to environmental/harmful chemicals today is likely to be 400 times more than exposure 50 years ago. A large study undertaken in the United States found that children between the ages of two and four years had the greatest exposure to harmful chemicals contained within, or on, the fresh foods they ate.[13] Pesticides used to protect the food from bugs were the biggest culprits, contaminating foods that children often eat, including tomatoes, peaches, apples, capsicum/peppers, grapes, lettuce, broccoli, strawberries, spinach, dairy, pears, green beans and celery. The American Academy of Pediatrics Policy Statement also draws attention to this and raises concerns about the additional toxicity of chemicals used to line tins and contained in wrapping papers and plastic containers in which food is packaged.[14]

While research about the effect of these chemicals on children's developing bodies and brains is limited, research using rats and mice has found that pesticides, fungicides and a range of chemicals associated with plastics — particularly phthalates and bisphenol A — can have concerning effects on gut and brain health, affecting the production of essential hormones that help maintain a well-balanced, stable level of function. Phthalates, used as softeners in plastics, and bisphenol A, released when a plastic is heated, have been found to cause behavioural changes in both male and female offspring. Different chemicals have different effects on the genders, but in general, research has found that there are increases in aggression, defiance, depression rates and there are decreases in attention, emotional control and inhibition.[15]

Natural food chemicals

Foods generally considered to be healthy may also be problematic to your grandchild, particularly if eaten in large quantities, and it's just so much easier for your grandchild to eat the same foods every day for an entire year of more. Fresh food has become available year-round instead of seasonally, exacerbating the build-up of food chemicals and the likelihood of food intolerance. Food intolerance can be to one or several different natural chemicals in foods, the most common being salicylates, amines, glutamates, dairy, and wheat/gluten.

- **Salicylates** occur naturally in tomatoes, strawberries, kiwifruit, avocados, sultanas and other dried fruits, citrus, pineapple, broccoli, tomato-based pizza toppings, tomato sauce and olive oil.
- **Amines** occur naturally, especially in protein foods such as cheese, chocolate, canned fish and processed meats.

- **Glutamates** occur naturally in tasty cheeses, soy sauce, yeast extract, hydrolyzed vegetable protein, soups, sauces, gravies, seasonings and many other foods. Reactions to these foods can vary widely in type and severity.
- **Dairy intolerance** is caused by the lactose (milk sugar) in cow's milk products. If a child is lactose intolerant, the first clue will be an upset tummy after drinking cow's milk. Poo may be runny and very smelly. The child may have dark rings around the eyes. You might also notice behaviour issues, mood swings and tantrums.
- **Gluten** is a protein found in wheat, rye, barley and often oats (this last one varies depending on the variety). Gluten intolerance (or its more serious cousin, coeliac disease) can cause abdominal pain, bloating, constipation, diarrhoea, weight loss and vomiting. It can also affect brain function. Child may lack concentration, tire easily and be more emotionally 'fragile'.

Food additives: flavours, colours and preservatives

A food additive is any substance that is added to food for advantage, for example to improve colour, appearance, taste, texture, to preserve food and prevent rancidity. Some additives are deemed useful as they stop decay of food and prevent bacterial contamination. Others provide no nutritional value, such as colourings and flavourings. In the United Kingdom in 2007, a key study was published in the prestigious medical journal *The Lancet*, which found there was hyperactivity of children in two age groups: three-year-olds and children eight to nine years of age. These children were 'normal' — not formally diagnosed with ADHD — but many displayed hyperactive symptoms after ingestion of six specific food colourings. This led to the United Kingdom and European Union recommending a voluntary ban of these six food colours. Australia and New Zealand's food custodian — Food Standards Australia New Zealand (FSANZ) — feels the research is not strong enough and, unlike the Northern Hemisphere countries, continues to advise no policy change, despite increasing evidence that thousands of families are experiencing a range of effects on their children (and themselves) including:

- irritability, restlessness, difficulty falling asleep
- mood swings, anxiety, depression, panic attacks
- inattention, difficulty concentrating or debilitating fatigue
- speech delay, learning difficulties
- eczema, urticaria (hives) and other itchy skin rashes
- reflux, colic, stomach aches, bloating, constipation and/or diarrhoea, 'sneaky' poos (poos that take a child by surprise — they don't get the 'feeling' they need to go to the toilet), sticky poos, bedwetting
- headaches or migraines
- frequent colds, flu, bronchitis, tonsillitis, sinusitis; stuffy or runny nose, constant throat clearing, cough or asthma.[16]

Unfortunately, and despite increasing evidence that certain chemicals may be harmful to children, the use of chemicals added to food has continued to skyrocket. Smaller, still developing bodies and brains make very young children more susceptible to harm and there are great concerns that these additives will be detrimental when ingested over a long period of time.[17] Many of the thousands of chemicals used in food have not been independently tested for toxicity and, more specifically, in children with long-term ingestion.

What can you do to help your grandchild's gut health?

The good news in regard to the gut–brain connection is that it is possible to change gut bacteria by changing a diet. In her own research, Dr Natasha Campbell-McBride, a neurosurgeon and nutrition specialist, found that changing a child's diet to include only natural, fresh foods — fruit, vegetables and meats, along with certain grains — can elicit a considerable positive effect on neurological health and development.[18]

A healthy diet is essential for every child's gut, body and brain, but if

you feel your grandchild does have gut problems, there are a number of specialists — nutritionists and dietitians — who can help get your grandchild's gut back on track. Focus needs to be on healing and sealing the gut wall to allow normal functioning and development to occur. Healing children's gut flora is much easier than for adults. If the gut lining is healed earlier, children are able to catch up in development or overcome behavioural difficulties.

- Consider talking with your grandchild's parents to ask if they would consider testing your grandchild off the foods that contain salicylates, amines, glutamates and diary and gluten, especially if you have concerns about your grandchild's behaviour or learning. It's best for the parents to seek support from a nutritionist or dietitian who specializes in this area. You can read more about the types of food that may be causing your grandchild's health problems here: **www.fedup.com.au.**

- If your grandchild eats a lot of any one food (like sultanas or strawberries etc.) and their parents agree that the behaviour is less than acceptable, then consider discussing with the parents its removal from the diet, along with other foods from the same group. Children usually react to more than one food chemical, so you may need to keep 'testing' by removing one type of chemical after another until you find all the culprits. Some aggressive children who are hyperactive respond dramatically to a diet that eliminates all food with chemical additives, artificial colouring, flavourings, preservatives and sugar. Others find that behaviour settles when one of the more 'natural' food groups is removed, such as salicylates, the most common food group to cause reactions.

- Your grandchild's nutritionist or dietitian may recommend probiotics that replace the normal bacteria to the gut, depending on the kind of gut challenges your grandchild may have. There are excellent products on the market for babies and small children. They may also recommend vitamin and mineral supplementation, as children with gut challenges may not easily absorb those necessary for optimal brains and bodies.

- Read labels and avoid food additives and preservatives. For a full list of the real 'nasties' see: **https://fedup.com.au/information/ information/additives-to-avoid.**

- Avoid processed food and 'fast food'. This includes processed meats. The more distant a food looks from how it looked when it was fresh, the more additives and preservatives it generally has and the more nutrients removed. Basically, this means that it's best to eat foods that have no additives — foods that are fresh, or fresh-frozen, unprocessed and unrefined. The old saying 'If it looks like something your grandmother wouldn't have eaten, avoid it' still very much applies!

- Wash all fresh fruit and vegetables *very well* before eating — not just a rinse under the tap. Most of these have been sprayed multiple times with anti-bug and anti-disease chemicals that are designed to 'stick', before they are picked. Research has found the most successful way to remove chemicals from fresh foods is as follows: Add 1 tablespoon of salt, or 30 grams (1 oz) of baking soda, to 3 litres (6 pt) of water. Soak your fruit and vegetables for fifteen to 20 minutes, then wash under fresh running water. You can use water and lemon juice on more delicately flavoured fruits like raspberries and blueberries.[19]

- Water should be your grandchild's primary drink once weaned. Filter drinking water if you can. Most water supplied in our cities is loaded with chemicals to stop nasty bugs growing, which is a good idea, but not so good for children's developing bodies. It is possible to filter out many of those chemicals, so children do not need to drink them. Some cities add fluoride to the water to help protect children's dental health. This is a controversial topic on which I will not embark, but be aware if you filter your water with a good quality filter such as a reverse osmosis filter, then you will filter out the fluoride. Activated carbon filters that attach to taps or fit into jugs usually only filter out chlorine and sediment, improving the taste.
- Avoid highly sugared, flavoured, coloured, carbonated drinks and 'sports' drinks. Offer pure fruit juices in moderation. It's actually better if your grandchild eats a piece of fruit. 'Reconstituted' juice drinks usually contain preservatives and other chemicals such as colours and flavours.

Further advice from the American Academy of Pediatrics Policy on Food Additives and Child Health suggest that families of young children:
- avoid microwaving food or beverages in plastic, including infant formula and pumped human milk
- avoid placing plastics in the dishwasher
- use alternatives to plastic, such as glass or stainless steel, when possible
- look at the recycling code on the bottom of products to find the plastic type and avoid plastics with recycling codes 3 (phthalates), 6 (styrene) and 7 (bisphenols) unless plastics are labelled as 'bio-safe' or similar, indicating that they are made from corn and do not contain bisphenols (recycling code numbers may vary between countries)
- encourage handwashing before handling food and/or drinks.

SUMMARY How well your grandchild's brain works depends on how well your grandchild's gut functions. Even if your grandchild is exceptionally smart, a poorly functioning gut will mean that he or she cannot reach their learning potential. Challenging behaviour is often the first sign that something is amiss with a child's gut health. It's worth taking the time, in conjunction with the child's parents, to try to work out if food or chemicals are problematic. The good news is that once the problem is solved and the diet changed accordingly, your grandchild will be happier and able to enjoy their childhood years to the fullest.

5

SLEEP SOUNDLY, ALL OF YOU

Your grandbaby or young grandchild will spend a large percentage of their time asleep. This need for long hours of sleep coincides with rapid physical growth, intensive brain activity and connectivity and emotional learning. In the past twenty years there has been an explosion in sleep research, showing that a good, long, regular night of sleep is the key to both physical and emotional health. But let's be realistic here: we all know the very last thing a new baby brings with it is a good night of sleep! Does this constant waking of the baby detrimentally affect their development? What about the wellbeing of the parents?

While I have seen the effects of lack of sleep on many children and families, I do not profess to be the expert in this area, so let's take a look at what the fascinating work of science tells us.

Why sleep is good for the brain and body

Professor Matthew Walker, a neuroscientist who has worked in the area of sleep for many years, has combined his research with that of many other experts in an excellent book called *Why We Sleep: Unlocking the power of sleep and dreams*. He convincingly argues that a good night's sleep is not

an 'optional extra'; rather, it is essential for the optimal operation and function of both brain and body. It is as important as food and exercise. And
not just a little sleep: at least eight hours is needed for adults and many
hours more for our younger generations. A good night's sleep enables the
body to rest and the brain to perform housekeeping duties that keep it
well-tuned and receptive for new experiences, to lay important memories,
and to be able to navigate the next day of emotional and social challenges.
Sleep has been found to be particularly important for the behaviour and
development of children.

What happens when you are asleep is really quite incredible. While the body rests, heart rate and breathing fall, muscles relax, gut movements slow down and we become unaware what is happening in the environment around us. The brain begins the great daily 'clean and tidy-up', getting ready for the next day of new information and experiences. The immune system reinvigorates, our appetite is regulated, blood sugar levels are stabilized and bacteria levels in the gut are maintained, so the body is also readied for optimal functioning. Importantly for your grandchild's developing brain and body:

- Sleep enables the constant modification of the architecture of the brain. During sleep the brain is able to reorganize itself while it is effectively 'offline'. The brain appears to sort through the day's information, sends some to long-term memory storage, strengthening neural pathways between different parts of the brain, while at the same time discarding unwanted information and removing unused circuitry.[1]
- During sleep, neural (brain) activity quietens down, blood flow decreases to the head and a watery liquid called cerebrospinal fluid (CSF) flows in and out through a system of 'drain pipes' (called the glymphatic system), washing the brain. This is thought to clear the brain of waste products that are generated by the neurons, and which would otherwise build up and irritate the brain, causing neurological problems, or, in the long-term, Alzheimer's disease.[2]
- Sleep ensures memories are consolidated so that new information and skills are sorted and 'filed' in the appropriate areas of the brain, allowing insight and problem solving. Even a short daytime nap helps with memory consolidation.[3]
- Sleep helps with the retention of newly learnt skills, so simple tasks can be recalled as young as 15 months.[4] Preschool children who sleep long and soundly at night have been found to have a more precise recall of newly learnt skills than those who do not.[5]
- Sleep is essential for the creation of long-term memory.
- Motor skill learning is consolidated and enhanced when children

get a good night's sleep.[6] My granddaughter reports that she rides her new two-wheeler bicycle 'in the day and in the night'. It's obvious that while she sleeps her brain is busy consolidating the new patterns of movement, balance and coordination needed to ride her bike expertly, and she even remembers her dreams about it!

- Genes responsible for the restoration of important neural (message) pathways are only turned on during sleep.[7] When sleep is shortened or disrupted, the activity of genes changes, affecting metabolism and immune responses. Lack of sleep has also been found to damage the physical structure of genetic material, affecting lifelong health and wellbeing.[8]

- A regular good night's sleep helps behaviour and reduces stress and anxiety. Poor sleep can increase the response to emotional stressors, with sleep restoring the balance in emotional centres within the brain, particularly the hippocampus, amygdala and prefrontal cortex. Sleep reprocesses emotional experiences and prepares for future emotional responses.[9]

- A regular good night's sleep helps long-term learning and behaviour.[10]

- Good quality sleep is particularly important for young babies and children as it has a profound effect on early sensory development and the creation of permanent brain circuits for the primary sensory systems. Sensory systems that require sleep for healthy development include the senses of touch, motion, position, hearing, smell and taste — a key way babies and children learn about themselves and the world around them.[11]

- Never has the saying to 'sleep on it' been proven truer! Research has found that the ability to come up with new and creative ideas and solutions to complex problems is increased threefold by a night of good sleep.[12]

- Children who sleep longer have been found to have a higher IQ and do better in school.[13]

How much sleep do babies and children need?

Children and adults alike need a good night's sleep, consistently. Babies and very small children need nearly twice as much sleep as adults. The following chart outlines the basic sleep needs of all ages.

Age	Hours of sleep necessary for a healthy brain
Babies under 4 months	14–17 hours
4–12 months	12–16 hours
1–3 years	11–14 hours
3–6 years	10–13 hours
7–12 years	10–11 hours
12–18 years	9 hours
Adults	8 hours

Sleep like a baby

Babies need a lot of sleep — ideally 14 to 17 hours a day. Their rapidly growing brains and bodies use a lot of energy. Yet the reported variations in how long and how well babies sleep are as numerous as there are babies. Some babies have a regular sleep–wake–feed–sleep cycle soon after birth; others take longer to find their 'rhythm', while others 'fuss more' and sleep is a scarce or short event. Science tells us that it is not until a baby is about three or four months of age that the internal 24-hour clock, or day–night rhythm (circadian rhythm), starts to develop enough for a baby to begin to settle into a more 'household friendly' pattern; and even then it is not matured until twelve months of age.[14] By around four years of age the circadian rhythm directs a child's sleep behaviour and most children sleep through the night, perhaps with a short daytime nap.

The good news is that while babies have a night of sleep interrupted for feeding, no effect on development has been shown.[15] It's likely that the parents suffer more from the lack of sleep over many months, and it is not uncommon to hear of fraying tempers or increased frustrations as they struggle to cope with their own sleep deprivation. If you have time, often the very best grandparent 'thing' you can do during these early months is to offer to help with household chores, or look after older children so your own children can grab a few extra hours of sleep when baby does.

Your daughter/daughter-in-law will decide just how she wants to sleep her baby. She may decide to co-sleep, or she may decide to sleep the baby separately in a bassinet or cot. Both have advantages and disadvantages, but that is a decision for your grandbaby's parents to make. If babies are sleeping in a separate bed, they should sleep on a firm mattress with a tightly fitted sheet. They must be able to lie flat. Car capsules (when not in the car), strollers, infant carriers and infant swings should not be used for sleeping as the curled position could compromise breathing.[16] Car seats/capsules should only be used in the car. If you are gifting your children a bassinet or similar, I highly recommend you purchase one that sways or swings. The swaying motion helps stimulate the vestibular system, calms the emotional system and helps your grandbaby sleep more soundly for longer periods.

It is highly recommended that babies sleep on their backs. Back-sleeping has been found to reduce the chances of an apparently healthy baby dying unexpectedly from Sudden Infant Death Syndrome (SIDS). While the 'Safe to Sleep' (formerly known as 'Back to Sleep') campaign has dramatically reduced the incidence of SIDS, sleep challenges have been amplified as babies 'wake themselves' when they are startled while asleep. The Moro reflex, an automatic primitive reflex that causes a rapid response to sudden movement, light or sound, is present until the baby is about eight weeks old. It causes the arms to fling out, the baby to take a sharp intake of breath and to start crying, waking the baby up. To help prevent this from occurring, swaddling, or wrapping, has been found to reduce wakening periods.[17]

If your grandbaby sleeps better wrapped, take the wrappings off when baby is awake. Swaddling a baby restricts movement and this reduces the time your grandbaby has to wriggle and learn how to move themselves. Once your grandbaby can roll over, swaddling should no longer be used for sleeping. Unwrapped, barefooted and mitten-free tummy time is important when your grandbaby is awake; it not only reduces the chance of a 'flat head' that can occur in babies who spend too much time on their backs, but it also gives them the freedom to dig their toes into the mat, see and wriggle their fingers, move their limbs and develop muscle tone and strength in readiness for moving.

Some babies may not settle as easily or as well as other babies. Many may still have immature guts (see Chapter 4, 'Guts and Brains') that are not coping well with the milk they are drinking. This is commonly referred to as 'colic'. Colic can occur as a result of ingesting either mother's milk or infant formula. Babies born by caesarean section are particularly at risk of colic, as they are not exposed to their own mother's birth canal bacteria at birth.[18] While most guts mature by around six to eight weeks of age (and sleep has been found to help this process), some need extra help. It is also possible that your grandbaby has food allergies or intolerances, and this should be seriously considered given the rising incidence in our youngest generations. Your grandbaby's doctor may recommend 'baby probiotics' that help 'populate' the gut with the right kinds of bacteria, and the breastfeeding mother could be recommended to stop certain foods known to cause baby's 'colic', such as dairy products, citrus, caffeine, some spices, stone fruit and certain vegetables such as Brussels sprouts, cabbage and cauliflower. Food allergies and intolerances need to be ruled out as soon as possible. The sooner you get on top of these, the sooner everyone in the household will be calmer and happier!

Sleep, behaviour and learning

The news about the lack of sleep in young children older than one year is not good. How well, and how long, your grandchild sleeps has both short- and long-term effects on behaviour and learning. Ongoing, insufficient sleep has been linked to increased tantrums or 'emotional meltdowns', anxiety, attention deficit, aggression, bullying and behavioural problems in children across all ages.[19]

It is thought that reduced or disrupted sleep, especially if it occurs at key times in development, could have important impacts on health throughout life.[20] In contrast to babies, young children (between one and two years of age) who sleep for shorter periods have been shown to have poorer thinking and language skills at two years of age.[21] Night-time sleep duration, compared to daytime sleep duration, has been found to have the greatest effect on the developing brain.[22] Furthermore, a lack of sleep has a cumulative effect, so a child who experiences irregular bedtimes and a poor quality of sleep over several years is more likely to have learning problems at school and be more prone as an adolescent to use drugs and alcohol. Insufficient sleep has been shown to adversely affect attention, impulse control, hyperactivity, working memory, reasoning abilities, risk-taking and emotional control.[23]

A study of almost 9000 preschool-aged children showed that those who averaged fewer than nine hours of sleep per night were significantly more likely to show impulsivity, anger and overactivity and to have tantrums than their peers who averaged more nightly sleep.[24] The children with less sleep were also 80 per cent more likely to show aggression. Although the study could not prove that lack of sleep affects behaviour, the outcomes do suggest that the length of sleep is critically important to a young person's health and wellbeing. However, another study found that children who averaged fewer than nine hours, 44 minutes of sleep per night (11 per cent of the participants) had higher odds of having all six of the behaviour problems examined compared with children who had more hours of nightly sleep.[25] Behaviour problems included aggression, tantrums, impulsivity, anger, annoying behaviours and overactivity.

The same study also showed that irregular bedtimes throughout early childhood can impair the development of thinking and learning. It was particularly notable that irregular bedtimes at three years of age were associated with lower scores in reading, mathematics and spatial awareness in both boys and girls at the age of seven. Furthermore, the impact is cumulative — so a child who experienced irregular bedtimes over a number of years was more likely to have learning problems at school.

It is also notable that many children diagnosed with ASD or ADHD have great difficulty falling asleep and then staying asleep. Professor Walker suggests that the symptoms that trigger the ADHD diagnosis are exactly the same as those that occur from a lack of sleep: inability to maintain focus and attention, difficulty learning, behavioural challenges and mental health instability. He furthermore points to the effect of drugs given to children with ADHD as causing even further sleep problems. These drugs are stimulants that are known to prevent sleep and keep the brain wide awake. While he is careful to say this might not be the case for all children diagnosed, sleep is something to seriously consider both as an aggravating factor and as part of therapy.

There are many reasons why your grandbaby or grandchild may be reluctant to go to sleep or sleep poorly. Children can sometimes have a sleep-breathing disorder caused by enlarged adenoids and tonsils. While in the 'old days' these would be surgically removed, they are now treated much more conservatively (i.e. they are left to 'grow out of it'). Unfortunately, these partially block the airway and this reduces the amount of oxygen that can be delivered to the brain during sleep. A child must wake up regularly to take several deep breaths. This prevents the child from reaching the deep sleep phase that enables the brain to do its night-time 'jobs' properly, resulting in chronic sleep deprivation over time. They often end up with symptoms similar to ADHD. Removal of the swollen tissues has been found to substantially improve sleep quality and symptoms often resolve spontaneously.[26] How do you know if your grandchild has this problem? They snore loudly!

Sometimes children won't settle to sleep simply because they have 'FOMO' — a fear of missing out, especially as they become more aware of what is going on around them. A toddler or preschooler can get mighty cross and refuse to go to sleep if they think they are missing out on the fun! They may also simply not be tired — if a preschool-aged child has an uncommon afternoon nap, he or she might not be tired at the time their 'usual' night-time routine dictates. Sleep can also be disrupted if in an unfamiliar environment or if care is being given by unfamiliar people. Food intolerances may cause gut pain or disturbances, or a child may just be hungry or thirsty. Sleep can also be disrupted if your grandchild is unwell or has a full bladder. Stress and anxiety can also have a major effect on settling to sleep and sleep quality.

Poor sleepers: the role of anxiety or stress

Babies and children who are highly anxious usually find it more difficult to settle and stay asleep. Babies who feel insecure, or whose mothers were exposed to high stress during pregnancy, especially the last twelve to fifteen weeks, may have higher levels of stress hormones in their blood, making it harder to relax and fall asleep. They may also have their Moro reflex still active after the eighth week of life.

The Moro reflex is a primitive reflex response to danger. It is designed to help an infant survive the first weeks of life. It is the earliest 'fight or flight' response, causing the stress hormone, cortisol, to quickly arouse the body. If the mother has been very stressed in pregnancy, her cortisol levels rise and so too do the baby's. The baby is then more sensitive to stress and cortisol levels are likely to remain high, instead of falling quickly after a stressful event. The Moro reflex response continues to be activated past eight weeks of age and the baby or child remains on 'high alert', making settling and sleeping more difficult. Because these children are on 'high alert', their senses are also highly alert. They may be hyper-sensitive to touch, light, sound and/or movement. This means they can be super reactive to the feeling of a rough sheet or the tag in their pyjamas, a flickering light, the hum of an airconditioner or fan, or even the feeling of rolling over in bed — making it very difficult to fall asleep and stay asleep.

If your grandbaby or grandchild is anxious, fretful and unable to settle to sleep, it can help to try to calm their emotional system. While loving cuddles and support are important, there are several other ways of helping:

- Consider your grandchild's diet. Are they intolerant to certain foods? This can really irritate the gut, the brain and the emotional systems (see Chapter 4, 'Guts and Brains').

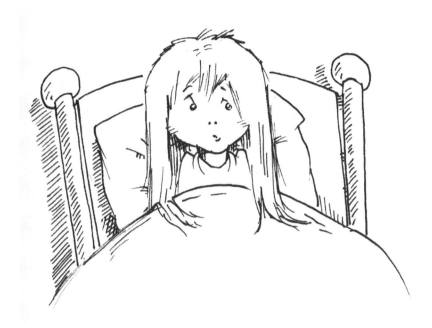

- The Moro reflex is activated by sudden head movement, touch, light and sound. It can be calmed and regulated by input from the sensory system, particularly the vestibular system, which is essential for balance and the body's response to gravity and position. Activities that help the vestibular system mature also help inhibit the Moro reflex. Daily opportunities for slow rocking, swaying, swinging, spinning and rolling can help.[27]
- Massage stimulates the sense of touch, calms the child and helps reduce the circulating stress hormones. A massage can be included as part of the bedtime routine. A warm bath prior to the massage is also calming.
- Active movement opportunities during the day are essential. Movement helps the vestibular system mature and enhances the production of 'feel good' hormones, endorphins, and reduces the production of stress hormones.

Dreams and dreaming of the 'wild things'

It is highly likely that your grandbaby started dreaming somewhere in the last two trimesters of pregnancy, but we are often unaware of our grand-children dreaming until they are able to verbalize their experiences. My own granddaughter, at around the age of three years, told her mother on waking one morning that she had been 'watching TV on the inside of her eyelids'! She had been dreaming about jungle animals after reading about them in her library books the day before.

Dreams are a very important part of sleep. This is a time when the brain consolidates memories, moving them from short-term storage into a long-term filing system, to be recalled when required. This period of sleep dreaming, called rapid eye movement, or REM sleep, occurs on and off throughout the night, but peaks in the early hours of the morning.[28] REM sleep is thought to be fundamental to long-term memory, learning, creativity and emotional regulation.

As your grandchild's imagination develops during the day, so too does imaginative dreaming occur at night. The popular children's book *Where the Wild Things Are* by Maurice Sendak provides a vivid interpretation of a young boy's monster-filled dream. Max is sent to bed without his dinner because he is cranky and irritable. His dream sails him off to dance with the Wild Things, monsters who behave badly. Eventually, he returns home presumably to sleep soundly and, just as science tells us, he will wake up in a better mood. My granddaughter has, over a period of several months, moved from an enjoyable dream phase of 'TV on my eyelids' to waking in the night afraid and inconsolable about the monsters and 'strange things' invading her dreams. She has no memory of these dreams when she wakes in the morning, and the day commences happily and positively. If your grandchild is staying overnight, it is useful to be aware that nightmares and night-time fears are very common in young children. Girls are more likely to experience them than boys. It has been reported that up to 75 per cent of preschool and young school-aged children experience nightmares, some having them more frequently than others.

Bad dreams and nightmares are thought to be the result of the brain

trying to make sense of a lot of new information, sorting out the 'good' from the 'bad', the 'useful' from the 'trivial' and the 'must keep' from the 'throw away' pile of the previous day's memories. Even as adults we can experience these very same bad dreams as our brains drag us through the torment of weird, wonderful and nonsensical thoughts.

While bad dreams seem to be part of a healthy, normal brain, they can be exacerbated by what's going on around your grandchild at any given moment. Stressful situations can certainly intensify bad dreams. If your grandchild is staying overnight with you, he or she may be afraid to be separated from you, they may be unfamiliar with the different sleeping environment, or the unfamiliar noises, lights, shadows and 'bumps in the night' could cause them great fear. While most children outgrow their nightmares, it can sometimes persist into middle childhood and affect sleep, learning and behaviour. Children who have ongoing high levels of anxiety are more likely to have persistent nightmares.[29]

Children who watch television or other forms of electronic media prior to bed may be at greater risk of having nightmares, particularly if the show they are watching has 'scary' parts in it. Yes, even animated movies or cartoons have scary parts — scary for the child.

To help reduce nightmares:

- Consider the food your grandchild is eating. Food chemicals, additives, flavours, colourings and preservatives can irritate the brain and increase the risk of nightmares.
- Ensure your grandchild does not watch TV for at least two hours before bedtime. Sit with your grandchild when they watch TV so you know what they are watching. Vet TV programs very carefully. You will be surprised at what scares them. Even the most 'harmless' of shows could contain frightening elements to the young mind. The same reminder applies to books.
- Make sure the room is cool or the fan is on. Sleep quality reduces and the likelihood of bad dreams increases when children get too hot in bed.[30] Do not overdress your grandchild or place too many blankets on top of them. It's better to have two blankets rather than one quilt/duvet, so one can be kicked off by the sleeping child. Natural fibre blankets such as wool, cotton or bamboo 'breathe' better. Don't tuck the bedding in too tightly. Children (and adults) can often be seen attempting to cool off their core temperature by hanging their arms and feet outside of the bedding.
- Make sure your grandchild goes to the toilet before bed. A full bladder is unsettling and may stimulate a bad dream.
- Have a night light or hall light on, so your grandchild can see if they wake up. The light should be dim and not LED. The blue light of LED stimulates the brain into thinking it's daytime.
- A warm bath before bed helps relax and cool the body core ready for sleep. However, if you live in a hot part of the world, children may prefer a cooler bath or shower.

Bedwetting

It is considered 'normal' for children to wet the bed up until around five years of age. However, children who are still bedwetting once they start school are at a great social disadvantage, as they are afraid to sleep over with friends. So, while it is not necessarily considered problematic if your preschool-aged grandchild is still wetting the bed, it's best to try to resolve it before school starts.

Bedwetting occurs when the sleeping child has a full bladder but the mechanism to wake them is not well developed and so they pee while asleep. While there are strategies, such as making sure your grandchild goes to the toilet before bed, there is also the possibility that they still have a primitive reflex — the spinal galant — affecting their nervous system messaging to the bladder.[31]

The spinal galant is a reflex that is stimulated by lightly stroking down one side of the lower end of the spine. This results in the hip flexing towards the side where the back was stroked. The opposite hip flexes when the back is stroked on the other side. This reflex is thought to help the baby wriggle down the birth canal, and when a baby lies on their back this causes the hips to flex, allowing the legs to kick, freeing them up for movement. This reflex should be de-activated by nine months of age. If it remains active it is thought to hinder bladder and bowel control, and just the light touch of bedding may stimulate it, causing bedwetting long after your grandchild is toilet trained.

You can test for the spinal galant by asking your grandchild to kneel on all fours and, with a pen, trace down the left side of his or her lower back, then repeat on the right side. Did your grandchild dip their back or move their hip on the corresponding sides? If the answer is yes, they may have an active spinal galant. Here are a few movement-based activities that can help that reflex disappear and stop bedwetting:

- Massage the lower back and hips every day.
- Play creeping games. Creeping helps move the hips, stimulating and freeing up the muscles of the lower back.
- Ask your grandchild to roll over and over, and from one side to

the other. Make it a game. 'How far can you roll? Can you roll like an egg, a ball, a log?'

- Ask someone who is strong to lift your grandchild upside down from the feet. This helps the back muscles extend. Children love being upside-down.
- After the age of three years ask your grandchild to do activities while lying on their back. For example, pushing themselves along by the feet and wriggling like a flipped-over beetle.

Bedwetting may also occur as a result of high stress levels and emotional insecurities. Helping your grandchild feel safe, loved and secure, a regular routine and a 'never-mind' attitude when accidents happen will go a long way in supporting a good night's sleep.

HOW TO ENSURE YOUR GRANDCHILD HAS A GOOD NIGHT'S SLEEP

- Enjoy lots of active movement during the day. Young children who are physically active for a minimum of three hours during the day will fall asleep more easily and sleep more soundly. Active children have a better quality and length of sleep than inactive children.[32]
- Have a regular bedtime. Let your grandchild know that it is bedtime and stick to it. If your grandchild is only with you during the day and still has a regular daytime nap or two, try to stick to the routine of sleep time as much as possible. Apart from the fact that you will notice a huge difference in behaviour and coping skills, your grandchild will also be able to concentrate and 'take things in' more easily.
- Implement a bedtime routine, so your grandbaby or grandchild knows what to expect when they 'sleep over' at your house. A routine might look something like dinner, bath, teeth,

toilet, story time, cuddles, a song and 'good night'.

- Try to have a special place for sleeping and keep to the same location and bed each time. Keep the room as dark as possible, and cool during warmer weather. Make sure the bed is comfortable and the room inviting and quiet.
- If your grandbaby or grandchild has a special comforter, or uses a dummy/pacifier to settle, then make sure these are handy. Some families use 'white noise' to help filter out loud noises from outside. This is okay to use while settling baby to sleep, but research (on animals) has found that it may affect hearing and subsequent language development if used for many hours at a time.[33] Discuss with the child's parents.

- Do not expose your grandbaby or grandchild to bright light (LED) before going to bed, such as in the bathroom. Have a night light for little ones who do not like the dark, or so they can see if they need to get up to go to the toilet.
- Avoid all screens if you can in the hours leading up to bedtime.
- Read a bedtime story to induce the natural calming rhythms of the brain and body.
- Avoid sweet, coloured drinks such as cordial and soft drinks/ sodas, especially in the hours before bed.
- A good night's sleep helps everyone manage the many challenges and tasks we encounter in our busy days. Children especially require the right amount of good quality sleep, as their brains are working extra hard at 'wiring and the firing'.

6

TALK, READ, PLAY —
AND BE A
TECH DINOSAUR

I think I can safely say that we all want our grandchildren to be capable communicators and competent readers. A competent reader not only reads words fluently, but understands what they are reading and, eventually, is able to critically think about the text. In today's world where 'fake news' and online 'facts' are questionable, critical thinking is an essential skill. I'm sure it will come as no surprise that the first steps towards critical thinking start with communication, language development and reading, and these begin long before your grandchild enters school; in fact, they start before birth.

How early your grandchild communicates, talks and how many words they have learnt by the time they start school depends on many factors, including genetics, the environment, illnesses (especially those affecting the ears and thus hearing) and sound experiences. While children's communication, speech and language development occur within a predictable pattern, there is great variation between when children master these skills. Some children seem to 'soak 'up language and master these skills very easily, while others seem to have more difficulty learning language concepts.

There are lots of games and activities you can play with your grandchild that encourage language and speech development, but first let's break down the components of what makes a 'capable communicator'.

Speech, language and communication

It is commonly believed that the terms speech, language and communication are different ways to describe the same set of abilities. Although these abilities are interconnected, speech, language and communication are fundamentally different and require the development of a distinct set of skills. In short, speech is the verbal sounds we sequence together to create words in order to talk to one another. Speech is a motor-based skill that requires not only complex messaging systems operating between visual, auditory and oral sensory systems, but the precise motor control of facial and tongue movements that enable the clear pronunciation of letters and words.[1]

Language is the meaningful way in which we sequence words into sentences to relay either a verbal or written message. It is important for social connectedness and relationship building. Communication is how we exchange information and ideas between people. It is also a motor skill, be it through verbal or non-verbal means. Verbal communication occurs through speech and singing; non-verbal communication includes reading and writing, body language or signing.

For the part of the brain that enables speech and language to function well, it is important to have good connections with the rest of an efficiently functioning brain, especially with the motor and sensory parts. Talking and learning to talk requires very complex motor planning. It requires the ability to initiate a motor act on an inner command.[2] To make sounds to form a word, specific muscle movements of the throat, mouth, tongue and lips are needed for articulation.

The connection between motor development and speech is highlighted when children have language difficulties. Children who are delayed in their speech development often have motor development delay as well.

There is also a link between oral language ability and speech skills, and the development of literacy skills and learning. Three-year-old children who have delayed or disordered speech and language skills will often go on to have literacy and learning challenges at school. This happens because when children lack a strong foundation of speech and oral language skills to build upon, it becomes very difficult to master the more complex skills required to encode and decode a visual symbol system (i.e. reading and writing). Unfortunately, as most of the academic curriculum relies upon the child mastering literacy abilities, weak literacy skills place a child at increased risk for poor academic achievement.

Reading to your grandbaby and young grandchild, singing and playing musical songs, games and nursery rhymes is a great way to promote language development and help lay the foundation for communication and learning to read and spell. Neuroscientists have found that hearing and repeating words, and moving rhythmically to music, teaches the brain how to communicate. It connects the necessary neural pathways children need in order to begin to speak and is encouraging for verbal communication. The more books read daily to a child during the first four years of life, the greater their language and speech skills by the time they start school.

Speech and language: start early

It takes time for your grandchild to build up the language skills and repertoire to be a competent, capable communicator, and much of this learning happens in their early life. We know this because children who regularly engage in direct conversation with adults as preschoolers are more likely to have greater language and communication skills when they start school, than those who don't.[3] So don't shy away from lots of talking with your grandchildren — just remember to pause and let them respond, so you allow them the opportunity to practise language themselves! This conversational 'my turn, your turn' back and forth is a great way to encourage the development of speech and language right from birth.

Language exhibits a 'critical period' (read about this in Chapter 1) of brain connectivity between birth and seven years of age, when the brain is more receptive to sounds than it will ever be again. This means young children can more easily acquire languages than they can later in life (see 'Multilinguistic grandchildren' on p. 115).[4] Even more specifically, the brain is most receptive to speech sounds *before* eleven months of age. Dr Patricia Kuhl, an internationally renowned psychologist from Washington State University, has intensively studied the development of language in babies, publishing many papers on her research about early language and bilingual brain development. She has demonstrated how early exposure to language alters the brain and how this then flows onto later language development.[5]

Why are the first eleven months of life so important to language and speech development? In the first months and years the brain is building the 'neural architecture' specific for each language. All babies between the ages of six to eight months are able to distinguish between different sounds in different languages. In one of her studies, Kuhl found that American nine-month-old babies exposed to Mandarin (twelve sessions of 25 minutes each, over four weeks) by native speakers playing and reading to them, were able to learn differences in sounds in Mandarin equivalent to native Mandarin speakers. Importantly, social interaction was a key factor to learning sounds and language. Another group of 32 babies who were exposed to Mandarin by watching native Mandarin speakers on a DVD or audio only, *did not* improve Mandarin sound distinguishing ability. Kuhl also found that by ten to twelve months, babies were already becoming attuned to their own language and 'culturally bound listening begins'.[6]

Infants listen to the frequency of sounds. 'Parentese' or 'motherese' uses a higher frequency of pitch that is much more interesting to babies. Slow, paused, elongated speech with sounds exaggerated make speech clearer to babies. The more parentese a baby hears, the more a baby babbles. The more a baby babbles, the better their ability to distinguish sounds. Babies who have a good ability to distinguish sounds at eight months have better speech and language at 30 months than those whose ability to distinguish sounds at eight months is poorer. Kuhl also found that infant sensitivity to vowel contrast sounds at seven months was positively correlated to language performance at five years of age. Children who start low at seven

and twelve months show a decreased ability in receptive and expressive language at five years of age.

Multilinguistic grandchildren

If you are a native speaker of a language other than the one your children and grandchildren speak, then please use every opportunity to speak with your grandbaby or grandchild in your native tongue. Ideally, it is the only language you should speak when chatting with your grandchild. An infant's brain is *so* receptive to the sounds of language that *by the time babies reach their first birthday, they will have learnt all the sounds needed to speak their native language or languages, if they are exposed to them.* Toddlers and preschoolers can also learn more easily than older children and adults. A young child's brain is not just limited to learning one or two languages but can adapt to manage multiple languages if regularly exposed to them.

I have a friend who is Hungarian, married to a German, and who has a Russian mother and a Polish father. They lived in Australia for three years when their two children were babies and toddlers. The children's language fluency was slightly delayed, and at four years of age both boys created their own language by combining the easiest words from any language in one single sentence. At six years of age both children spoke Hungarian, German, Polish, Russian and English — with an Australian accent! They also had a small amount of French and Italian as they went there for holidays. The youngest was very upset when, at eight years of age, they visited Croatia and he could not understand or speak the language. However, by the end of their four-week holiday, he was conversing with the locals in their native tongue. The power of the young brain. Amazing.

Communication and conversational 'turn-taking'

How well children verbally communicate is important for both health and learning. Children who have good communication skills are more likely to be successful in the classroom, be socially happy and more able to regulate their emotions. As adults, good communicators are more effective, and happier, in their occupation and life.

There is much evidence to show that conversational turn-taking between an adult and child is the way children learn language, but conversation is important for much more. Conversation includes speaking, listening and thinking and, in combination, these lay the foundations for learning and literacy skills in a number of important ways.

Language development

From birth children are surrounded by a world full of language. As they begin to develop their own oral language, the influence of the adults around them makes a world of difference to just how much language they develop. Hearing others speak begins the process of learning how language works. They learn the sounds of words, how they fit together, the rhythm of the language and the correct context in which they are used. The development of learning to listen and speak is crucial not only for academic learning, but also for social and emotional growth. Conversations are an important way to enlarge vocabulary.

Relationship-building

Your grandchild is learning about life every single day. One important lesson is how to begin and maintain healthy relationships. Your relationship with your grandchild serves as a model for future relationships. Engaging in rich discussions teaches your grandchild how to be an active participant in life and that how they talk, listen and think about what others are saying has a direct impact on friendships. This is particularly relevant to grandchildren older than three who are starting to interact and play with other children.

Discovery of the world

Talking with your grandchild creates an opportunity to reveal something to them about the world around them. For example, while going shopping, conversation might reveal how food is prepared by finding appropriate ingredients for a recipe, or how to create a shopping list and follow through with it, or even learning about different cultures. For your grandchild, everything is a lesson and conversations are one vehicle in their learning process. Once children turn three this discovery is often accompanied by a lot of questions! 'Why?' is a common refrain, so take the opportunity to give a simple explanation if you can. 'Because' is not an answer that will satisfy this curious age group!

Reasoning

Conversations encourage your grandchild to think about new ideas, develop questions and make decisions. It is so important to encourage your grandchild to think and make decisions for themselves. This helps them become more independent and self-sufficient. If your grandchild is over two-and-a-half years old, let them choose their own clothes to wear. Ask questions like: 'It's a hot day today, what clothes do you think will be best?',

'It's cold today … it's windy and raining today …'. Prompt them to think about things they may not remember … 'Do you need a hat?', 'Do you need shoes or sandals today?'

Understanding diversity

Your young grandchild is naturally self-centred. They see the world as revolving around them. Through interaction with different people, children learn that there are many different kinds of people with differing ideas, life-styles and opinions. They then begin to develop understanding and accept-ance of differences. Rich and frequent conversations with a wide variety of people can even teach your grandchild how valuable diversity and discus-sion can be, as we each have something special to contribute.

Reading

Children who are often read to in their early years are found to have an increased vocabulary and are more likely to enjoy reading at school. Researchers have found, through MRI technology, that reading to young children causes activity in the brain related to reading skill development, verbal development and image development, giving children a cognitive advantage early on. In their study, Dr John Hutton of Cincinnati Children's Hospital Medical Center and his colleagues were able to see the actual activity that goes on in the brain when they read to young children.[7]

The researchers found that children who were read to more frequently at home had more activity in the area of their brains that helps derive mean-ing from language. This area is essential to verbal language development and ultimately reading. Children with more opportunities to hear complex grammar also have higher activation in the area of the brain responsible for speech. They also found that brain areas associated with mental imagery were strongly activated, allowing children to develop visualization skills — the ability to 'see the story'. Well-developed visualization skills are crucial to academic success.

Reading to your grandchild is also a precursor to enjoying reading at school. Reading out loud encourages an interest in books and reading, and stimulates the development of many cognitive skills, providing essential building blocks for later learning. Don't stop reading out loud when your grandchild starts reading by themselves. Reading out loud is enjoyed by children into their early teens and is brilliant for developing visualization skills — a skill not practised when watching TV or screens. Visualization is the ability to form a mental picture in our mind's eye. It is a thought process that enables us to create or recreate imaginary or real actions or scenes. We can visualize with our eyes open or closed, while we

think about or remember something, or read a book and imagine the characters or scenes. It helps us make sense of, and enjoy, what we are reading.

Every time you read a book you are visualizing, even though you are unaware of the process. You create your own images in your mind (visualize) of key characters, how they sound, look and move — helped by the author's descriptions. You become very aware of this when you head to the movie version of the book … and come out thoroughly disappointed! The leading actors look, sound and move nothing like you had imagined! I deliberately avoid movies of books I love. I'm almost always disappointed by the director's interpretation of lead characters. I prefer my own visualized heroes and heroines. Not surprisingly, everyone visualizes a different interpretation of the same book because how we visualize is based on our own life experiences. The more life experiences and reading aloud opportunities we provide our young children, the more practised they become with visualization skills and the more likely they are to enjoy reading.

INTERESTING FACT

Children under six read whole words as pictures (using the right side of the brain). After six years they begin to decode and can sound out letters and words (phonics, using the left side of the brain).

What are the best books for babies and toddlers?

Reading to your grandbaby or grandchild is one of the most relaxing and enjoyable activities you can undertake. They will love the rhythm of your voice as you move through the pages and enjoy the visual stimulation as pictures flick by.

For babies' visual development it's best if books have pictures of a single object with sharp contrasts or a bold outline. However, when it comes to auditory, speech and language development the truth of the matter is you can actually read anything you like to your grandbaby! Using a sing-song voice, read out loud whatever you fancy, including weekly magazines or the local paper. If you are interested in a particular field of study, why not read your books out loud? Quantum physics, Shakespearean prose, human anatomy, psychological theories, environmental issues, wildlife articles and business management are all interesting to your grandbaby!

Older babies and toddlers are starting to pay more attention to basic, simple images. They love 'lift the flap' and feely, textured books with hard cardboard pages that are easy to turn. Preschoolers love stories with funny parts or interesting animals, or that tell a tale of adventure, albeit a simple one. They can scan quickly through quite complicated pictures to find the smallest, almost hidden detail, and they start to notice if you miss a page or a few words!

If you do, however, want ideas about great books for babies and toddlers there are some terrific ones available today — ideas abound online and in your local library and bookshop. The local library is a great free resource so enjoy regular visits there — the children's books are usually plentiful, and you and your grandchild will enjoy a wonderful time of book discovery together while you make significant long-term contributions to their language and thinking skills.

Screens and communication skills: be a 'tech dinosaur'

In contrast to face-to-face communication and reading to your grandchild, screens and electronic toys have been found to hamper the development of good language and communication skills.

One study involving parents with babies ten to sixteen months old found that electronic toys may slow language development in toddlers.[8] These expensive toys may be advertised as 'educational' for developing minds, however the study found just the opposite. Each family was given three sets of toys based on three themes: animal names, colours and shapes. The first set included electronic toys such as a baby laptop, a talking farm and a baby smartphone. The second set contained traditional toys such as wooden puzzles, shape sorters and multicoloured rubber blocks with animal pictures. The third was a set of five board books of which three provided lift-the-flap opportunities. All sounds were recorded to monitor the play activities. The results showed that while children were playing with electronic toys the parents spoke less. There were also fewer verbal exchanges between parent and baby and the parents responded less often to their child. The babies were also less vocal and produced fewer words while playing with noisy electronic toys than when playing with traditional toys. It was found that books produced the most verbal exchanges between parents and their children. The study also demonstrated that play with traditional toys may result in verbal interactions that are as rich as those that occur during reading a book.

You might notice that when your grandchild plays with electronic toys that make noises or light up, their attention is very focused. These toys are extremely effective at commanding children's attention by activating their orienting reflex. This primitive reflex induces the mind to focus on novel visual or auditory stimuli.[9] Toys with noises and flashing lights may be appealing, but they could prevent children from engaging in the world around them and from explorations that make their learning more meaningful.

The regular use of small screens and mobile devices is also detrimental to the development of your grandchild's vision. For healthy development children's eyes need exposure to natural sunlight and to practising long-distance viewing. That means being outside to play. Professor Molina, an optometrist who lectures in clinical optometry, has warned that if we allow our very young children to use screens on a regular basis they will join the 50 per cent of the population who will need glasses by eight years of age.[10] Scary thought? Indeed it is! However, there are ways to avoid myopia (short-sightedness).

Importantly, we need to heed the warnings of those researching and working in the area of vision and eye development, and the very first step we need to make is to take control of our own grandchildren's screen use. Professor Molina recommends the only way to protect children's eyes from long-term damage is to say an absolute *no* to device/screen use in children from birth to three years. The young child's visual system is still developing, and eyes are being trained for optimum use. From three to six years of age a one-hour limit *weekly* should be imposed, and between six and twelve years, 2 hours maximum *weekly* will not cause long-term harm to our children's eyes. Of course, we all know this is a very hard ask, but perhaps while your grandchild is with you it may be possible to avoid screens for that period. In my household, and even though we are a very tech-orientated family, when my grandchildren are with me all screens are off and stay off. I'm happy to be a 'tech dinosaur', and to be honest, painting with real paint, reading real books, playing picture, card and board games or going to the park is *way* more fun!

However, there is one caveat to this 'banning of screens'. I admit to using the video function of my phone to speak with my grandchildren on a regular basis. I cannot always be with them and this style of face-to-face technology means I can stay in touch on a more personal level and my distant grandchildren know me better. While it is not as good as being there, it is wonderful to watch them grow and to be able to stay in touch this way.

Several of my friends use this technology to read stories to their grand-children at the end of every day, or to 'attend' birthday parties and other important family occasions.

Play and the development of communication, speech and language skills

The best way to stimulate language and communication is through play. As you have read above, you don't need special games and toys, and if you have not moved away from your long-time family home you may still have a lot of the games your children played stored away somewhere. Well, it's time to bring them out! The more traditional the toys your grandchild plays with and the more stories read out loud, the more words they will be exposed to. Play doesn't even require expensive toys; grandparents, you are actually the best 'toy' your grandchild will ever have. Your grandchildren will learn a lot of language skills when they share play activities with you, and you just need to open your cupboards to find the best and cheapest play activities. Pots and pans, a blanket for 'peek-a-boo' and a basin with water or cooked spaghetti are wonderful tools for play and language development of grand-babies. Toddlers and preschoolers love 'helping' in the kitchen, the garden and the workshop, and while you won't actually achieve much, it's a great play opportunity for them.

Play helps develop vocabulary and listening skills and helps develop the ability to follow directions. As language becomes more complex, play also develops and games become more complex. For grandbabies, play means activities like banging objects together, putting objects in their mouth, examining objects. For grandtoddlers, building with blocks, pushing cars, blowing bubbles. For preschool-aged grandchildren, pretending to feed a doll, talking on a pretend phone, doing pretend cooking or building a zoo. Play is the way children experience their world and the world of others. As a grandparent, playing with your grandchild provides you with a window into their developmental stage and challenges. It's also fun!

Playing with traditional toys helps to increase attention span, encourages imaginative role-play, exploring options and solving problems. Exploring options is at the heart of lateral thinking. Creative children feel free to propose alternative solutions and are keener to follow their curiosity. Children learn to take risks and experience the value of making mistakes as part of the play process. Traditional toys provide opportunities for children to express all their wonderful ideas. Toys like building blocks and puzzles can help develop spatial intelligence, important for learning mathematics later. Playing with traditional toys can teach the social skills of taking turns and accepting and respecting others' leads.

When children have the opportunity to play traditional games, they also stimulate the muscles of their eyes and their vision. As they move from one place to the next, their eyes learn to adjust — near and far, up and down, from left to right and back again. The brain is also learning to interpret what is being seen. These are essential skills for learning to read — eyes need to move smoothly and in unison across a page to read, and the brain needs to be able to interpret what is being read. This ability to visualize and perceive, or understand, what we are seeing, are key ingredients to learning. Children with limited movement opportunities often find these tasks much harder.

Dr Jeffrey Goldstein, co-founder of the International Toy Research Association, claims that the decline of interactive play between adults and children using traditional toys in favour of electronic toys has resulted in an increase of sensory issues and emotional problems in young children.[11] The more hurried lifestyle, changes in family structure and increased attention to academics and enrichment activities means that children today experience less time playing with their families than previous generations. When children under the age of six spend much time playing with electronic toys, it takes time away from play with toys that are vital for the stimulation of the sensory systems and development of motor skills, crucial for developing their brain and wellbeing.

Grandparents, this is where you come in! Parents are often so rushed as they manage their busy days, but when you care for your grandchild you have the perfect opportunity to provide these very important missed opportunities. It is your soothing voice, your soft, unhurried touch and your loving gaze during play that will make a significant imprint on your grandchild's brain. Playing with your grandchild creates joy, intimacy, self-esteem and openness while building those essential neural pathways and connections that will be needed for later learning.

PLAYING WITH YOUR GRANDCHILD: ACTIVITIES AND IDEAS

BABIES

Your grandbaby is learning the sounds of language and how to replicate them, from scratch. While having heard sounds in utero, they were muffled and often distorted, their own mother's voice being the clearest sound heard. At birth, hearing is the most well-developed sense and your grandbaby's hearing is better than it ever will be again in their whole life, so the more exposure they have to the sounds of language or languages, the better.

- Face-to-face communication is essential for developing communication skills. Speak face to face with your grandbaby and small grandchild and give them a chance to respond – even if it is only with babble or nonsensical verbal sounds. Use the 'my turn, your turn' method: you say something directly to your grandchild (they must be looking at you or, if blind, be aware of your presence, right with them) and wait for them to respond. Do not rush into further conversation. Babies really have to think about, and process, an oral response. But they can do it! Practice and time are important.

- Do not expose your grandbaby to screens. They learn nothing about language and communication from a non-responsive picture. However, if you live away from your grandbaby and use video technology for face-to-face communication, this is another matter entirely. Video technology enables you to respond to your grandbaby in an interactive way even if you are thousands of miles away.

- Read to your grandbaby from birth. Babies love lyrical, rhythmical prose, although what they love most is your voice. If you read the most boring of textbooks to a baby in a sing-song lyrical way, they will love it, regardless! Read simply illustrated books. Black outlines on a white page are great. If you have any of the Dick Bruna series still in the cupboard from your own children, these are perfect. Simple, one dimensional, clearly outlined drawings are ideal for your grandbaby.
- Talk to your grandbaby using a sing-song voice whenever you are doing something with them or to them — massaging body parts, exercising, dancing, playing with musical instruments, changing nappy/diaper or clothes, etc.
- Sing and play action rhymes and body movements with your grandbaby. Nursery rhymes are ideal.

TODDLERS

Your grandtoddler is still in the 'motor development' phase of learning and wanting to move dominates their brain. While some may have a collection of words, others will have only one or two, such as Mama, Dada, dog, duck, etc. Don't let this stop you building their repertoire of words. Just because they are not saying them doesn't mean they are not learning them. My own granddaughter had few words at two years of age, preferring to mime everything (pointing was popular), but as her motor skills improved and her brain matured at nearly three years of age, her speech exploded. She quickly started speaking in sentences, using words like 'tarnished' (Santa's boots in *The Night Before Christmas*) in the correct format and with the correct meaning. Needless to say, she has not stopped talking since! She talks all day and into the night as she goes to sleep. This is a very common story, so keep the language stimulation going even if you feel you are the one doing all the talking.

- Keep up the 'my turn, your turn' process of conversation. Toddlers will respond, albeit that they ask you to watch them as they retell something that has happened to them, or that they would like to do, through action only.
- Talk about concepts and encourage your grandtoddler to move their body in these ways: up/down, around, in/out, over/under, etc.
- Sing and move to music and encourage participation in rhymes and action songs.
- Talk about something you have done together. It may be about simple household chores or activities in the garden.
- Read lots and lots of books. Books need to be simply illustrated and have few words as toddlers have a short concentration period and your grandtoddler will want to turn the page quickly. 'Lift the flap' and 'feely' books are popular in this age group.
- Encourage the use of a wide range of words that might not be commonly used at home – bob, jump, up, down, balance, upside down, right arm, left arm, right leg, left leg, etc. Touch and move the body parts or do the actions as you talk about them. The brain learns words much more effectively if it can link a movement or action to the sound.
- Avoid screens. Communication skills deteriorate with too much screen time as children do not practise their own speech when sitting and staring at a screen.
- Tell stories without books – imaginary stories not only help imagination, but language skills are developed as well.
- Sing songs, play music and move to the music by following the instructions. Talk it through out loud.
- Laugh and play fun games.

PRESCHOOLERS

- Play verbal memory games – place three or four common household objects on a tray. Ask your grandchild to look at them, tell you verbally what they are, then cover them up and, without your grandchild looking, remove one. Ask: 'What's missing from the tray?' Start with three objects, removing one. Build up to six objects and remove two or three if they find it easy.

- Ask questions: 'Can you do this? Can you show me how? How can we do this in a different way?'

- Link words to action: 'Can you show me how to jump? Hop? Gallop? Walk sideways, backwards? Dig? Walk like a dog, cat, tiger, elephant, giraffe, penguin?' etc.

- Ask children how they feel: sad, angry? Encourage them to express verbally how they are feeling. Say the words, express in sound.

- Activities that combine thinking and moving help with language development as preschoolers learn to follow verbal instructions and complete more complex tasks, e.g. 'Can you bring me two forks and three spoons?', 'Can you put on your right sock and right shoe? Now can you put on your left sock and left shoe?'

- Talking about their experiences of the day is a great way to help children learn to visualize and to recall and explain verbally what they did. They do need help with this and learning by example helps. So, tell them about your day. This shows them how to 'sum up' the highlights of the day's activities. Then, ask them about their day, using prompting questions: 'What did you do when you went to …? What did you see? What colour was …?' etc.

- Tell stories about your own childhood and about your grandchild's parent's childhood. This is likely to stimulate lots of questions from your preschool-aged grandchild, so be prepared for 'What's a ...? and 'What does it look like?'

- It's never too early to link the sounds of words to the written word and images, and by three years of age children can begin to recognize the 'pattern' of the word (not the individual letters, but how the word looks overall), often referred to as 'whole word' learning. Use picture books with single words for each picture. The 'old-fashioned' Ladybird picture books were excellent for this if you can lay your hands on a set. You and your grandchild can also make your own books. Using craft paper, fold a number of sheets together to replicate the pages of a book. Find pictures from old magazines that can be easily associated with a name — for example, a picture of a cat or a dog, household items, wild animals, etc. Ask your grandchild to cut out the picture and paste it on the left-hand page. Print the word on the right-hand side (facing page) so that it is big enough for the child to read (about font size 40 to 44). You can make different books on different topics.
- Music and singing are excellent for the development of language skills. This age group can learn the words and sing along to the music.
- Stick to the topic. A conversation has a natural and organic progression that works best when it is not forced or dictated but followed. Sticking to a topic means discussing a subject through to a natural stopping point or digression. Sometimes sticking to the topic means accepting when and where it changes.
- Listen effectively. Ask interesting, thoughtful and thought-provoking questions. Focus on your grandchild and nod your head to show them you are listening and interested. Use sounds of encouragement, like 'hmm' and 'uh ha' at the appropriate moments, so you show how to be attentive. Not only are you listening to your grandchild, but you are showing them how to listen.

- Join in the imaginary games played by your grand-preschooler. They are fascinating and you will be surprised by your grandchild's capacity to visualize many different scenarios and life experiences.
- Listen for your grandchild's interests. This helps you to steer the conversation to topics they are comfortable and enthusiastic about.
- Be yourself, because conversing is a two-way street and you want your grandchild to feel at ease and comfortable. Be open, engaging and generous.
- For your older grandchild, elaborate by adding details and description to conversation as this makes it more interesting and clearer for your grandchild. Use descriptive language and concepts to help describe things.
- Use positive body language. Body language is a very important part of helping people interpret what is being said, and children are very tuned in to body language from a very early age. Good eye contact and an appropriate tone helps a child interpret and respond to your topic of conversation, and in turn tells your grandchild that you are interested in theirs.
- Include concepts in your conversation – up/down, in/out/ around/through, etc., and move in these ways. These elements of language also form the basis of writing and mathematics.

7

MAKE MUSIC, SING, DANCE

What a treat! An opportunity to write a whole chapter about one of my passions — music for young children. Fortunately, music happens to be a key element in developing well-skilled children and this section will explore this with a focus on the smart things you can do to create an environment conducive to optimal development in your grandchild.

It's hard to imagine a world without music, especially a preschool world. We use music as part of our celebrations and rituals, we use it to add intensity to images in film and it is used to calm or excite shopping environments. Marketers know about the power of music to sell products and we all know the effect of a song that we associate with a particular event. Music affects us on an emotional level, and is often used to support us through emotionally challenging times. Songwriters use music to heal emotional pain and people going through similar experiences use those songs to ease their own situation. Although there are aspects of the internet and this digital age that are challenging for people working with children, in our modern society we have easy access to a huge range of music in a way that was not available to our own grandparents.

However, this discussion is about children, how music helps development and what part music can play in a well-rounded educational environment. When you observe children participating in musical activities their engagement and enthusiasm is obvious. We have talked about movement, nutrition and sleep as essential elements in development, but music fits comfortably with these 'super brain foods'. These four elements nourish the brain, and all play an important part in helping brain maturation.[1]

So, where does the musical journey start? Right from their time in the womb, where a baby is tuned into the rhythmic beating of their mother's heart, voice and associated noises. They are listening to a tailormade version of 'My Mother's Symphony'. Parents use gentle rhythmic movements to settle their newborn babies, they sing to soothe an upset child and they play music to their children. If you already have a grandchild, remember the first time you held that child: there was probably a strong urge to rock, bounce or sway the new baby, especially if they were a little unsettled. It is a hardwired response and we know it works.

What does music do to the brain? It is known through the use of MRI technology that music stimulates the brain, with studies showing a larger auditory section of the brain in musicians when compared with non-musicians.[2] But there are also studies that have shown these effects are not limited to the auditory abilities. When children listen to or participate in music activities many parts of the brain are used for a range of processing associated with music, such as memory, attention and motor skills. Music also stimulates the limbic systems and associated emotional responses. However, not only is the brain stimulated, but there appear to be some lasting effects on our ability to think.

Cognitive abilities, which is the 'technical speak' for thinking abilities, appear to be influenced by musical activities. Research by Professor E. Schellenberg showed an increase in children's IQ when they participated in music lessons for a year. His study involved 144 six-year-olds who were randomly assigned to music lessons, drama lessons or no lessons. Through a battery of testing he found that the children who were in the music lesson group (keyboard or vocal) had a larger increase in their IQ than the children who participated in drama lessons or no lessons.[3] Studies conducted by Professor Frances Rauscher and Dr Sean Hinton and their team at the University of Wisconsin, Oshkosh, showed that children aged four years benefitted from weekly music lessons.[4] Tests that required the representation, analysis and mental manipulation of objects showed that the children who had received music lessons performed better than children who had not received music lessons. However, they were very clear that children must participate in the music activity to gain the cognitive advantage — just listening to music does not produce the same increase in brain function. Other studies have shown improvements in academic achievement.[5]

Music and pregnancy

Listening to music and singing, along with regular movement activities, has been shown to help babies' development even before they are born. Mothers who sing to their babies, actively move and who eat a healthy diet during pregnancy are not only healthier themselves, but so are their babies. Research conducted by Professor Michael Lazarev over 35 years with more than 30,000 pregnant mothers, has shown that in-utero babies exposed to daily singing, music and movement are born with enhanced physical, mental, social and emotional maturities compared to babies whose mothers had not participated in the program, and they continued to score more highly on developmental checklists until the commencement of school (when data collection stopped).[6]

How does singing and moving help an unborn baby grow?

While the exact mechanism of stimulation by the mother and response by the foetus is not clearly understood, Dr Alfred Tomatis — famous for developing sound therapy, which has helped thousands of people improve their hearing and understanding of what they are hearing — argues that the foetus listens with its whole body. He proposes that music sets up a certain vibration, which results in a full body, physical reaction that is very stimulating to the developing brain and body.[7]

An unborn baby's motor development is enhanced through the mother's movement that, in turn, stimulates its own movement. 'Movement-sensing' neural pathways of the growing brain are formed and operational from eight weeks in utero. This movement-sensing system, called the vestibular system, is the first sense to be fully operational. While it takes many more years of movement experiences for the vestibular system to be fully matured, even in its early stages of development it is responsive to movement and the brain is recording every move the mother and baby make. This lays key motor pathways for later developmental skills.

When music and movement are combined, the effect on the developing brain is magnified. The sense of hearing and the vestibular system are located in the same part of the body — the ear. The vestibular system is located inside the inner ear, in an area called the semi-circular canals. Fluid washes over tiny hairs that tell the brain in what position the head is located or moving in — up, down, left, right, forward, backward, or upside-down. When the senses of hearing and vestibular, in combination with movement, are stimulated, the brain receives lots of wonderful information about rhythm, beat, sound patterns and motion. The more information the brain receives from the senses, the better it is at learning to 'making sense' of the information it receives and the better its ability to appropriately respond to that information, even at this very early stage in development.

Other developmental stimulation occurs when in-utero babies are exposed to music and movement. Rhythmical patterns of musical sounds lay the basis for the inborn sense of rhythm. An inborn sense of rhythm helps with the development of language and movement and enables the child to 'fit in' with the 'rhythm of life' that goes on around them — an innate sense that children with ASD (autism spectrum disorder) do not have. Music also prepares the ear, body and brain to listen and understand the sounds, enhancing not only the sensory system, but also understanding, thinking, intelligence and learning.

Singing and moving in pregnancy are also great for the mother's mental health. They help to relieves stress, enhance the mother–baby bond and create positive emotions.[8] Communication also develops between the mother and baby, promoting emotional maturity through early bonding. Singing has also found to enhance bonding with dad and grandparents if they sing to bub.

Now you have some theory as to why music is such an important

component of a rich environment. However, let's take a look at what an enhanced musical environment looks like and how you could contribute to the development of your grandchild.

Music: participation is best

Music for children can be about listening, but the best quality music is all about participation. When children are moving and using their senses the experience is much richer. Having the child involved as early as possible is always my aim. Initially, they just mouth the instruments. But of course through all the sensitive nerve endings in the mouth they are gathering information; they gather more this way than using just their hands. Adding a percussion instrument to a recorded song extends the experience, especially if the child is involved in the playing. I have recorded lots of music over the years, and I have always seen it as a means to getting children involved whenever I can. However, I too used music in the car as entertainment. It was very useful.

Keeping the beat

For all children, regardless of age, the ability to keep a steady beat is a fundamental skill. Many more advanced skills are completed more easily and successfully if the person has a strong sense of the beat. This does not just relate to musical activities, although it is very helpful — many sports have a beat or rhythm associated with the set of skills required. Cycling, athletics and rowing are obvious ones, but horseriding, football, table tennis and skating also require a sense of timing and rhythm. Some games require these skills, such as tiddlywinks and pick-up sticks. But within the school environment, there are activities both academic and social where a sense of rhythm and timing help children join in with their peers. So there is nothing trivial about being able to keep a steady beat.

In my years of teaching music classes with young children, I have often said that one of my main functions each week is to find as many ways as I can to keep the beat, for as much of the session as I can, in ways that the parent and child do not tire of. If I spent 45 minutes each week tapping some sticks or just banging a drum my classes would empty out pretty quickly. However, if you carefully analyse all the activities I do, you will find a steady beat is a common element. My children can keep the beat while walking, lying down, sitting in odd positions, with a distraction such as a beanbag on their head and with a wide variety of percussion instruments. But this does not happen overnight, and they often started as babies with an adult who knew about the value of keeping a steady beat.

Dance is a powerful way to let a baby feel the beat. So dance with your grandbaby! Hold them in your arms, put on some music you like and dance, making sure you emphasize the beat by gently bouncing. When they are young babies your bounce will be small, but as they get older you can get more bouncy. Music from the 1960s and 1970s often had that very strong beat — the songs where the dance floor quickly filled are often the ones. Some examples that work well are *Hooked on a Feeling* (Björn Skifs), *Sweet Caroline* (Neil Diamond), *My Guy* (Mary Wells) and *Walking after Midnight* (Patsy Cline). But you will have other favourites. The good thing about choosing something you like is that the dance will be emotionally satisfying for you and your grandchild will sense that. Make sure that the beat is not too fast and that you can comfortably dance to it.

Those of you who have a musical background may have noticed there has been no mention of rhythms so far. Children pick up rhythms and patterns through the language they are hearing and through the music they listen to. However, when they are young if they can establish a steady beat, then rhythms and patterns naturally follow and they do not need to be taught.

Sing with your grandchild

Live music is very powerful both for the musician and the listener. There is a very big difference between a live concert featuring an orchestra and a recording of that same orchestra. Much of that is to do with the vibration

you feel when the orchestra plays. Even with the best sound recording, this vibration is missing. Digitally produced music and recordings of live instruments sound different, there are small imperfections in the live instrument and, in my opinion, it sounds much nicer.

Singing is the same: nothing compares with beauty of a live singer. The very best musical instrument you have with you at all times is, of course, your voice. I can hear you saying, 'But I can't sing!' Children do not care if it is Dame Kiri Te Kanawa or Dame Joan Sutherland, their gran or grandad. It is the vibration in your voice that holds the power — so sing with your grandchild. Teach them nursery rhymes and make up little songs, just short rhymes with a tune that goes with regular activities you do. I had a 'Going up/down the stairs' song when my son was little as it was something we did quite often. We would arrive at the top or bottom of the stairs and

I could tell he was waiting for the song to start. Sometimes we went very slowly, sometimes it was fast, sometimes I sang it in a high squeaky voice or a deep, low voice, sometimes it was smooth or the words short and clipped! That simple little song covered many musical components in one short little trip. I notice my neighbour has taken the song singing I suggested with her granddaughter very seriously and she has a little song for lots of things they do. The delight on the child's face is clear to see and at four months old you can see the child recognizes Nan's song.

Sing a book

When you add music to reading you access different parts of the brain and this is a good thing to do. Singing stories can make them more memorable for the child and add another dimension to the story. I often sing books, but there are some tricks to making this successful.

Carefully choose the book you are going to sing. Of course, the very easy ones are nursery rhyme books as there is often a well-known melody that works with the pages of the book. When you have exhausted these, move to books that are not too long and have good rhyming. They are usually written with four lines that rhyme, so sometimes a well-known traditional melody will fit the words such as *Here We Go Round the Mulberry Bush*, *Twinkle Twinkle Little Star* or *Frère Jacques*. Then the next step is to make your own melody to a simple book. There are many books that fit this category such as *Rumble in the Jungle* (Giles Andreae) and *My Dinosaur Dad* (Ruth Paul).

Slightly more complicated books to sing are well worth the effort if you have the inclination. Some good examples include *The Very Hungry Caterpillar* and *The Very Busy Spider* (Eric Carle), *Dear Zoo* and *Oh Dear* (Rod Campbell), *The Little Yellow Digger* (Betty and Alan Gilderdale) and *The Waterhole* (Graeme Base). The problem is remembering the melody you sang; it is likely your grandchild will tell you if you are not singing it right. My suggestion is to work out a melody and record yourself so that you can remind yourself next time what you did.

Reading to children as if you are an actor on stage is a good idea, but adding music gives you even more room to shade and colour the story with variations in tone, pitch and intensity.

Music for your yet-to-be-born grandchild

As a grandparent, you are encouraged to sing to your unborn grandchild. It's something you can do while mother-to-be is visiting you and resting with her feet up. Ask the mother if she is happy for you to sing to her baby, and then sit beside her and sing. You do not need to sing to the tummy or get a megaphone, just sing, and the mother might even sing with you. You can sing anything but you may like to sing, such as things from

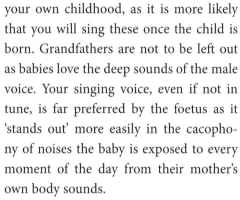

your own childhood, as it is more likely that you will sing these once the child is born. Grandfathers are not to be left out as babies love the deep sounds of the male voice. Your singing voice, even if not in tune, is far preferred by the foetus as it 'stands out' more easily in the cacophony of noises the baby is exposed to every moment of the day from their mother's own body sounds.

Very young babies appear to particularly receptive to the rhythm and rhyme of lullabies and nursery rhymes. There are many wonderful nursery rhymes and lullabies and they are easy to learn if you are unfamiliar with them. This is not to say that other forms of music are unsuitable for your developing grandbaby to hear, it's just that lullabies and nursery rhymes have special qualities that can benefit their development. Lullabies are calming melodies that replicate the rhythm of the heartbeat, breathing and the slow movements of the developing baby in the womb. Nursery rhymes slow down the patterns of speech and enable the vowel sounds of language to be more easily 'picked up' by the baby's developing hearing.[9] Once your grandbaby is born, they are likely to be very responsive to them especially if you have been able to sing the same songs repeatedly to your grandbaby over the course of the pregnancy. Repetition is an important way of giving the growing baby time to recognize the beat and the tune. It might also mean that after birth, your voice is recognized and a special connection made

MUSIC ACTIVITIES

Grandparents know that good quality time helps develop good relationships. Music is something that can use quite a chunk of time if young children are allowed to wander through the exploration of sound, rhythm and rhyme. Parents often don't have time to sit and bang the drum with the child for as long as the child would like to bang the drum! In their time-pressured world, a few bangs are enough and then they move on. Enter the grandparent.

BABIES
Music activities with babies mainly revolve around keeping the beat as has already been suggested. Sing songs in such a way that there is a very clear beat, and dance every day.
Develop a bag of interesting instruments. These may be instruments from your own or your children's childhood, but they may also be things you make or buy. I always keep an eye out for interesting instruments when I travel as different cultures make musical sounds using different and often interesting materials. But often you don't need to travel far to find them as fairtrade shops can be a good source of interesting instruments. I also always have my eyes on the lookout when I am in

a second-hand shop, as people often discard their children's instruments.

You can buy interesting shakers such as maracas or eggs, but homemade ones are great as well. Make sure the containers are not too big or have a way that the baby can hold them. Old plastic water bottles are a great size for your very littlest grandchild as they have a narrow neck and are light. Have several with different fillings: little pebbles, grain of some kind, seeds that are past their use-by date, dry leaves, little sticks, small cones or seeds from trees. Make some so that the child can see what is inside, and some that are hidden. Make sure they are light so the child will be able to shake them. Glue the tops of the containers with strong glue so that they cannot be undone.

TODDLERS

Toddlers do not often sit still for a lengthy musical session unless they are totally captivated by a live instrument or similar. So at this age it is 'music on the go' or music in the car. Make a box or bag with a range of instruments both homemade and manufactured, that you keep at your house or bring with you when you care for your grandtoddler. When you bring out the bag make sure you allocate quite a bit of time to play with the instruments and experiment with the possible sounds. Allow your grandtoddler to explore the instruments and also play them yourself. Although it may look like they are not taking any notice, trust me, they are. Their brain is sponging up everything you do and they find it hard to resist someone who is enjoying music, even if they do not join in immediately.

Continue to build your instrument library. The key components are:

- instruments you shake: maracas, bells, egg shakers, rain-makers

- instruments you bang: tambourine, cowbells, drums (home-made or bought) that make different sounds, used clean meat trays (with the ridges) are fun as you can bang them or stroke them with a stick and they can make very interesting sound
- instruments you manipulate: triangles, castanets, rhythm sticks (claves), boom whackers, washboard (I found a metal one of these in the United States – it is very cool)
- pitched instruments: xylophone, chime bars.

This is not an exhaustive list, but a good place to begin.

Follow the child's lead – when you can. If they make a pattern, copy it. If they play the instrument in a certain way, copy that too.

Add simple nursery rhymes to your instrument time. Songs and rhymes are useful for language development, especially if your grandchild speaks two or more languages. A very easy way to learn another language is through songs.

PRESCHOOLERS

Preschoolers who have had earlier opportunity to develop their musical skills can be extended at this stage. Make sure they can keep a steady beat by clapping, using other body parts (e.g. feet, elbows), walking and clapping or playing an instrument or more challenging moves like clapping behind the body or off to one side.

Once this skill is well established you can begin to play with rhythms. And of course, the easiest way to do this is with words. Dr Suzuki of the Suzuki Method of learning an instrument has this well embedded into his system.[10] The children play with words that make rhythms by clapping the syllables. I have several sets of pictures where the words help the children clap the rhythm. These sets can target a child's interest, be it a set of cards about transport (car, bus, tractor, scooter, helicopter and train), animals (cow, horse, lion, tiger, spider monkey, elephant) or another area of interest. Initially, the game is to find out how many claps are needed for each picture. Then the child will arrange the pictures in a line (usually only four at a time) and clap the pattern formed by the arrangement of pictures. It is easier to start and finish with one-syllable word. For example, cow, lion, tiger, horse is easier than lion, tiger, spider monkey, elephant! Save those for when they have got the idea. They can then progress to playing one of your instruments, playing different instruments each time through, having multiple four-line patterns, taking turns playing the pattern, and so on. The combinations are endless. The reason I have suggested you keep these patterns in groups of four is that 4/4 time or 'march time' is the easiest for children to learn. They pick up the beat earlier with this time signature, and there is a little bit of mathematics being developed as well.

The nursery rhymes you sang with them as a baby can now become a source of rhythm patterns. This is useful as a musical skill, but also good for literacy skills (yes, everything is linked).

Once they have this sorted, they can then start making their own music patterns that you can copy. These kind of games are all part of musical literacy and when children have these skills well established, any musical instruments they begin learning are so much easier due to the very solid foundation.

Remember to sing with your grandchild. Just your voice and the child.

Some grandparents even take their grandchildren to a music-based class or pay for the child to attend (a great Christmas or birthday present). At these classes, you can extend your musical repertoire and reinforce the activities at home. Also, keep an eye out for live musical performances aimed at children. Sometimes a local library will invite musicians to play for children, or the local orchestra will put on a short concert for young children. There is nothing more powerful for a child than the vibration/sound of an acoustic instrument. It is a multisensory experience. They are working out such things as where the sound is coming from, noticing changes in pitch and expression and how the music makes them feel. While you might not have this opportunity, your local school will also stage performances from time to time, so check with the school, as these are usually free concerts.

SUMMARY It is not hard to tell that I am a bit one-eyed when it comes to music and young children. However, the benefits are documented through research, and it is a fun, easy way to develop some very useful foundation skills for children. Time is the most challenging aspect for busy parents — taking the time to play musical games and being able to enjoy them. Music, like many of the things talked about throughout this book, is really beneficial when engaged in a small amount, often. I always like to ask, 'What has my child done musically today?' In my case there where little musical snippets throughout the day, so it was easy. We would stomp to the mailbox, clap to the clothesline, and during the 'learning to skip' phase not only was I told to skip down the supermarket aisle, but I had to sing as well! I am sure all the other shoppers thought I was completely barmy, but I reasoned that it was my child developing his skills, and who cares what they think! I certainly didn't.

I hope the message has been clear. Music is a powerful learning tool, especially when the child is a participator rather than a spectator. Simple, cost-effective musical opportunities provide a raft of foundation skills that will be in place for future scaffolding of other skills. What a wonderful gift to give your grandchild.

8

SPARKING CURIOSITY, IMAGINATION AND CREATIVITY

Human beings have a highly developed ability to creatively innovate, but to do this well requires curiosity and imagination. Having explored the previous chapters covering the essential elements of a healthy, well-functioning child, it is now time to go to the next level — developing the innovator, philosopher, creator and interpreter that is your grandchild. For me, this is where the real fun begins. This chapter explores the components of curiosity, imagination and creativity, and gives you simple ideas to use with your grandchild.

Curiosity

Young children are naturally curious. Once able to see well and deliberately reach out and grasp objects, your grandbaby wants to learn about the world around them as much as possible. When they reach for a toy, they look at it, feel it, listen to it, put it in their mouth to taste it and they try to move it and use it in different ways. Once mobile, babies actively explore every nook and cranny of their homes — unfortunately, often finding the hidden tiny dead insects that the vacuum cleaner missed!

Toddlers are unstoppable in their thirst for looking, touching, lifting, climbing, hanging on various rails (e.g. in the bathroom) throwing things and posting things. Note: beware! The toilet is a popular posting receptacle and toilet paper is fun to unwind off the roll! The toilet itself is also attractive and worth a thorough investigation. On one occasion when my daughter was distracted briefly, my sixteen-month-old grandson found it to be a great alternate source for water play, fortunately feet first, until he got both feet jammed in the narrow bottom and the fun ended! Needless to say, there is now a lock on the bathroom door.

Once they start talking, preschoolers ask hundreds of questions. What's that? Why? How many? Why can't I …? Who is that? Why does she look like that? What does she do? Why do worms help the vegetables grow … and on and on. They are willing to try different ways of moving: climbing over, under, around a piece of play equipment (or furniture), finding utter delight in their own successes. As grandparents, we need to help them realize their curiosity as this is how they actively learn about the world around them and how they stimulate creativity and imagination.

In recent times educators have realized that 'knowledge-based' education (learning facts that can then be regurgitated) is not very useful when most of us have online searching at our fingertips.[1] What we need are thinkers, people who look for creative solutions and are critical in their thinking, so that the issues facing our world now can be remedied. Children aged four to six years are in their prime when it comes to creative thinking. Remember, creativity is not just about the arts; it is essential for the progression of new ideas and ways of thinking across every area of learning. Of course, I believe the best place to begin developing these skills is with our preschoolers. I adore the clear thinking of a three year old as they explore ideas and concepts from their perceptions of the world. Three year olds

often say some very wise things, although some of them are also highly entertaining. I know a three year old who needed a shortened version to describe the act of sitting opposite someone to play a game. His solution? 'We need to be oppositting!' Perfect logic and a creative solution. Another example is that of little Miss Three. After a discussion about a consequence of death being that someone could no longer see or be seen by family and friends, the COVID-19 pandemic ignited her creative thinking skills. Her world, as she knew it, had been closed down and she said, 'Mummy, when we are alive again, can we visit Grandma?' A sentiment truly echoing how we all felt during long periods of isolation and social distancing, but one that made many adults smile. These examples show how children's application of creativity and imagination enables them to arrive at a solution or explanation. The key is to always look for what is right in their answers and build from there.

An early indicator of learning is curiosity. Curiosity drives attention and provides the emotional spark that ignites learning. Attention is fundamental to learning and if a child develops curiosity their attention improves as they want to do/see/understand more. One of the best examples of curiosity-based learning is the theory of Rudolf Steiner.[2] He believed that imagination and magical thought create a fertile ground for learning, and while our modern learning environment is focused on critical and analytical thought, imagination and curiosity are still the drivers of the motivation to learn.

Encouraging curiosity takes time and it is tempting to give the answer that you understand to be correct. However, the brain has a better workout when adults understand that it is good to allow the child time to complete the mental gymnastics being undertaken as they work to solve their dilemma.

Imagination, visualization and creativity

Your grandchild's imagination plays a key role in the development of curiosity and creativity. Imagination develops as she or he explores and learns about the world and encounters different experiences, objects, actions and outcomes. Imagination is the ability to mentally see in the mind's eye how things look, feel, smell, taste, sound or move and then to recall this information or apply it to a new way of thinking or doing. This ability is also referred to as mental imagery or visualization. For example, a child of three years old may be able to recall what game she played yesterday (or last week) and describe it to you in detail. She can do this because she recalls in her mind the images of the game. She may then be able to make up a new game, based on what she recalls from the game she played last week but using her imagination to change the rules or the actions.

Babies as young as seven to ten months have the capacity to create mental images. We know this because they recognize their mother within a few weeks of birth and can form a mental image of their mother's face even when she is not present. A one-year-old child can use mental abilities to post a ball into a circular hole, they love playing peek-a-boo, repeating simple rhymes such as *Round and Round the Garden* — they begin to anticipate the 'tickle you under there' so you know their brain is running ahead with the rhyme and remembering past experiences, or they can imitate a drinking action when wanting a drink. They also begin to enjoy a little gentle silliness (nothing too silly or concerning). Having a range of funny hats to try on yourself will entertain a child of this age. They know what you look like normally, and by adding something extra you are changing what they know or expect. You will know if they don't like the hat as they will take it off if they can, putting you back to what they know and like. I am very careful when I teach if I am wearing a wig with this age group (I am a sucker for a bright yellow wig when the focus is the colour yellow). I let them see me put it on, and then I only leave it on for a short time. The very surprised faces (right voice, wrong look) tell you that all is not well in their world. So go gently with this one.

Being able to create mental images is an important part of pretend play.

By the age of fifteen to eighteen months, your grandchild can engage in simple games of make-believe and games of pretend, initiated by others. By two years of age, most children can participate fully in such games. They begin to master the ability to picture, remember, understand and replicate objects in their minds that are not immediately in front of them. Early pretend play often consists of object substitution, using one object as a stand-in for another, such as block being used as a phone, or a cardboard box as a car. As your grandchild develops their mental imagery skills they gradually develop more complex forms of games that include using invisible objects, or imagining an article to be something else entirely — for example, a blanket over a table becomes a cave, or a chest of drawers a crocodile. By the age of three years, children can talk about people who are travelling, or who live somewhere else, such as Grandma in another town. By four years of age they can draw a picture of, or pretend to play with, a kitten that is not there. They can also talk about or draw places they visited, as well as create new scenes and creatures from their ability to visualize.

Visualization, imagination and creativity are especially evident in children's games of role play, where your grandchild will pretend to be a teacher, a parent, a gardener, a park ranger, a zookeeper, etc. This kind of imaginary play occupies a considerable amount of time from around two-and-a-half years of age, developing along with a variety of cognitive skills that include the imitation of others, perspective-taking (being able to put themselves in someone else's shoes), symbolic thinking (e.g. a roll of cardboard is a telescope looking at the stars) and planning ('I'll do this and then you do that, and then we …').[3]

The power and purpose of visualization and imagination cannot be underestimated. Not only does it drive curiosity and creativity, but it can also accelerate learning and improve performance of all sorts of skills. Brain studies reveal that mental imagery produces the same mental instructions as actions.[4] Just thinking about our body doing something (e.g. raising an arm or walking forward) directly activates the part of the brain responsible for movement. This ability allows us to remember and mentally rehearse our intended movements so we move more effectively. For athletes and

musicians, for example, going through the motions or mentally rehearsing the movements in their minds (or forming motor imagery) is effective for learning the exact movements required for a successful outcome. Even picturing others in motion warms up the 'action brain' and helps us figure out what we want to do and how we can coordinate our actions with those around us.

When children struggle to visualize easily it affects their ability to learn and hampers their performance in all areas — physically, academically, socially and emotionally. So it is important grandchildren are given the opportunities to develop this well before they start school. Reading, planning, understanding and communicating have greater depth when the

brain can retrieve past experiences using mental imagery. One research study found that eight-year-old students who were asked to create mental images during word memory tasks learnt two-and-a-half times as much as those who were told merely to repeat the words they need to remember.[5] Being able to visualize can enhance motivation, curiosity and creativity, improve motor performance, prime the brain for success and increase confidence and self-motivation.

Sparking curiosity and encouraging imagination

Understanding the importance of curiosity, imagination, visualization and creativity gives you the background to be able to make the most of your time with your preschool-aged grandchild while helping develop their skills.

Sparking curiosity in your grandchild is as important as engaging in active, everyday play. At home, you can ignite curiosity by:

- focusing on your grandchild
- being positive
- encouraging your grandchild to attempt a task, even if only part of a task
- actively participating with your grandchild
- praising them for a task attempted or achieved
- accepting the answers and observations they offer
- looking for what is 'right/correct' in their suggestions or observations
- resisting the need to put them 'right'.

If your grandchild is not engaged in the activity you are trying to interest them in, or appears to be focused elsewhere, perhaps you need to spark a sense of curiosity. Say to them 'Wow that looks fun', 'What can we do with this?', 'Come on, let's have a go'. At this young age, you do usually have to get involved in the activities with your grandchild, and they love having fun together with you.

Go outside (if you can)

Previous chapters have highlighted the importance of regular outdoor play. Health and development benefit from time outside as do creativity and curiosity. However, due to lifestyle changes, there has been a decline in the amount of time children play outdoors. A Norwegian study found that motor skills increased when children played in nature and a British study found links between increased self-esteem and increased social interactions when children played in the forest.[6] There has been an increase in the Forest School movement but there has also been a sharp decline in the amount of time children in the United States are spending playing outdoors.[7] Similar results are found in New Zealand and Australia.[8]

Dr Stephen R Kellert of Yale University states that direct experiences with the outdoors and nature are critical but ever-diminishing.[9] Kellert claims that nature is important to children's development in every major way: physically, intellectually, emotionally, socially and spiritually. Play in nature, particularly during the critical years of early childhood, appears to be an especially important time for developing the capacities for intellectual development. It also increases attention span. In a review of sixteen studies completed on 'nature play', researchers found that nature play had positive outcomes on health and development, in particular creativity, imagination and dramatic play, as well as developing social skills, emotional intelligence and creative thinking skills.[10]

When children have freedom in nature through unstructured, open-ended creative activities, they use their brains in unique ways as they come to understand new stimuli.

- Natural spaces and materials stimulate children's limitless imagination and serve as the medium of attention, inventiveness and creativity.
- Plants, stones and dirt present limitless opportunities for play, and that play can be expressed differently every time a child steps into nature.
- Children make up the rules and use their intelligence in their individual way.
- Nature is a natural attention builder. Often children who are restless and can't sit still are significantly more successful after time spent outdoors.
- Children can create their own world without labels, pre-conceived ideas and instructions. It promotes problem-solving.
- They learn to understand what works and what doesn't, what lines of thinking bring success or failure, how to know when to keep trying and when to stop.
- Time in nature helps children to note patterns, as the natural world is full of patterns and pattern building, a crucial early mathematics skill.
- They learn about similarities and differences, another skill for learning. Time spent playing in nature affords many opportunities for sorting.

- Play in nature often requires persistence. Children try and try again to see if their experiment works. If a branch doesn't reach across the stream or the bark does not cover their hut or fort, they keep trying until they succeed.

Outdoor play in nature offers evidence that children's mental development is dependent on experiences in nature. It builds a child's attention and learning systems and is therefore integral for cognitive development. Countries with the highest literacy rates in the world (Iceland and Finland) have outdoor daycare centres, which enhance child development through the provision of movement, touch, human connection and nature. Outdoor play in nature is stressed even in the coldest of weather. Learning in nature has a long tradition in these countries. In summary, get your grandchild outside whenever possible.

Abstract thinking questions

Once your grandchild is talking well, from around two-and-a-half to three years of age, it can be fun to start asking questions that require some simple abstract thinking and visualization. These questions stretch the child's mind — but only do this if you can accept the answer they give and resist the temptation to make it all about your knowledge and perceptions of the world.

Some examples of such questions are:
- Why do houses have windows?
- What makes the kettle boil?
- Why do cars have windscreens?

A three-year-old in a hurry to do something else told me that houses have windows so the cat can get out (the cat had just jumped out the window), and after very careful thought a two-and-a-half year old told me that cars have windscreens so you have somewhere to put your windscreen wipers — impressive! As an extension you can ask, 'Are there any other reasons?' Both these children took the information they knew and applied it to

the question. In both cases, I accepted the answers and they told me there were no other reasons. What they offered was 'correct' even if my opinion may have been different.

Imaginary play and creative activities

Grandparents can be very useful when it comes to imaginary play. Here are reminders of some simple, cost-effective things you can do with your grandchildren.

Storytelling

Storytelling is a wonderful activity for the development of language, thinking and of course imagination. Creating stories using imagination or retelling childhood memories is a wonderful way to extend visualization skills. Children love hearing funny family stories and they will want to hear them over and over. As an extension when they get older, story games are fun. In this game, one person starts a story and the next person adds the next line, then you add another line — hilarious at this age! You never know where you will end up.

A box of dress-ups

It is great if you have room to save a few things your grandchild can use when visiting. Old hats, cut down dresses (they love things that sparkle) or shirts, belts and a cape or two.

My son loved our dress-up suitcase and I was regularly at the supermarket with Spiderman or Batman in tow. Swords were the weapon of choice and he had one for every occasion (made out of wood or foam) with associated scabbard. My own mother was a little challenged about taking her Ninja Turtle grandson to town; she is always immaculately presented, but she managed to enjoy the creativity and got over the worry of being seen by anyone she knew. I also love meeting my neighbour's child in the driveway dressed as a firefighter, police officer or dinosaur to name a few. His grandmother really embraces his creativity and often has additions to her attire, suggested by her grandson, so she can be in character too.

My advice to you as a grandparent is to foster their creativity, as our grandchildren will need large doses of it for their futures. Never throw anything out until it has been assessed as a potential addition to the dress-up box.

Art and craft

These are powerful activities when developing creativity, visualization and imagination in children. Keep interesting boxes, containers, wrapping paper and ribbons, paper towel rolls, scraps of fabric, wool, empty cotton reels and similar. My ex-teacher mother-in-law had a treasure trove of things my son could use to create with. She enjoyed watching the creative process and the chat that went with the building process. He regularly came home with very complex constructions and a long, involved story of how it worked or what it could be used for. Imagination and creativity working at full strength!

Paint, crayons, paper, scissors and associated art materials might not be your thing due to the potential mess. However, a paintbrush and small bucket of water can provide endless fun outside if there is a fence or some concrete to 'paint'.

Making huts

This is another activity that provides endless fun for children. Set the parameters of what can be used — maybe provide some cardboard boxes (a cardboard fridge box is perfect for hut building) and blankets. Plastic picnic plates will enable meals to be created, and an imaginary cup of tea in a hut is always fun. These things take time but the rewards are worth the investment.

HOW TO HELP YOUR GRANDCHILD DEVELOP VISUALIZATION SKILLS

NON-MOBILE BABIES

- Start with tummy time on a mat outside so your grandbaby can see, touch, hear and smell the world in a new way.
- Read simply illustrated books. Black outlines on a white page are great. Simple one-dimensional, clearly outlined drawings are ideal for your grandbaby.
- Play with your grandbaby to expand visualization, so they can experience and experiment with sounds, sights, activities and feelings.
- Provide your grandbaby with a variety of toys to play with such as a rattle to shake, soft toys that squeak when squeezed, different textured toys that expand their know-ledge of how things can look, feel, taste, sound, smell and move differently from each other.
- Sing nursery rhymes using actions so your grandbaby feels the movement and develops a mental image of how the song sounds, and what the body movement feels like. *Twinkle Twinkle Little Star* is a popular nursery rhyme with babies and adults alike.

CRAWLERS AND CREEPERS

- Allow exploration inside cupboards, under beds, around the house and garden and especially with bare feet, so they can feel what they see.
- Read picture books out loud. Make sure the illustrations are simple. Make up stories.
- Play peek-a-boo. This encourages your crawler to remember that there is someone under the scarf and to visualize who it is. Note: crawlers don't develop 'object permanence' until around nine months of age … so younger babies will forget you are under the scarf!
- Have a special treasure box filled with everyday items that feel and sound different – like crinkly paper and a soft brush, large blocks of different shapes and sizes (which don't fit in the mouth), balls of different colours, textures and sizes, a bucket and spade (which can also be used as a drum), plastic containers, a rice shaker (dry rice in a small plastic bottle with a lid tightly on).

TODDLERS

- Set an obstacle course to engage them in a variety of movements and tactile experiences.
- Visit the local park, playground, beach, farm, zoo for a variety of sensory-motor experiences.
- Provide opportunities for messy play (if you can). Playdough, non-toxic finger paints, clay, mud, water and sand are perhaps best done outside where possible.
- Use different facial expressions, voices and touches to expand visualization skills.
- Provide sensory play using water, sand, mud, clay, playdough, paints, objects from nature.
- Provide different fabrics, papers, sponges with different textures and colours. Talk to your grandchild about how they feel and look.

- Read books, share stories and sing nursery rhymes using actions.

PRESCHOOLERS

- Listen to classical music and make music with percussion instruments.
- Encourage open-ended play with items such as blocks – a block can be a car, a phone, something to build with and much more; or use cardboard boxes as cars, trucks, trains, etc.
- Provide construction materials for creative play, and ask, 'What can you build?'
- Encourage your grandchild to practise their motor skills so they can build up a memory of movement patterns, and visualize and motor plan.
- Play with your grandchild to expand visualization, so they can experience and experiment with sounds, sights, activities and feelings.
- Allow for periods of 'free play' when your grandchild can use their imagination to play their own made-up game. They might want you to join in and be a pirate, a scientist, a crocodile hunter or a soldier. Whatever they decide, it's important you play by the rules of their game and follow them strictly! It is, after all, their mental imagery and imagination and you cannot possibly know what is in their head.
- 'I spy' is a great game for this age group, and even though they are not yet familiar with the letters of the alphabet, they can use colours, for example, 'I spy with my little eye something coloured green'. To extend imagination, you can always ask questions such as, 'Is it soft?' To which they must answer 'yes' or 'no'. Keep asking questions until you can guess correctly.
- Ask questions about their day. What did you do? Who did you see? Where did you go? What did you wear? How did you get there? This encourages them to recreate the visual images in

their mind and then verbalize them (quite a hard skill for this age group).

- Go for nature walks and look for collectable craft. Patterned leaves, flowers, bark, sticks, moss, etc. I take my nearly four-year-old granddaughter on walks around the block regularly to stock up her craft box. Her fourteen-month-old brother loves to come along as well and also contributes to the craft box (although be prepared to carry the younger ones most of the way home). She has begun to notice that the trees have different 'seasons' and that leaves change colour and flowers come and go. On our most recent walk she said, 'Next time the

frangipani has flowers I'm going to collect heaps to make a necklace for mummy.' Her imagination and creativity are blossoming alongside her knowledge of how the world works.

Visiting places with your grandchild

Building a bank of information is helpful for children, and visits to real workplaces provide a wonderful source of information for the creative brain. Take time to watch what is happening and give the child opportunities to ask questions. Going to visit Daddy or Mummy's workplace is something we might not necessarily think of as important, but until your grandchild has been there they cannot imagine what their parent's workplace looks like or what they do. So if you are caring for your grandchild while parents work, try to organize a time when you can visit, even if just for short time, perhaps spanning over lunch break so everyone can enjoy lunch together. Some workplaces have family days especially for this very purpose.

While visiting a parent's workplace is important for building mental imagery, visits to other workplaces are also suggested — museums, airports, aquariums, a local food manufacturer that has tours for children, etc. With today's health and safety laws it is harder to get into factories and other workplaces but do the best you can. One of my glorious moments according to my nephew, Jack, was a 'surprise' outing I took them on. We got in the car and I said that they could tell me which way to go to see if we could find the surprise. Jack knew about left and right so he took charge of giving directions. He still marvels, at 28 years old, as to how *he* managed to get us to the Air New Zealand maintenance hangar where there was a man who showed us round. He thought it was magic or his cleverness, or just amazing luck … It was a wonderful time that they have not forgotten. However, other outings were not as successful, like the day I took another nephew to an animal park. He made fleeting glances at the passing animals while maintaining his almost complete focus on the wheels of the tractor pulling the trailer we were seated on. I tried to distract him with giraffe feeding, but in the end, we spent most of our time on the trailer with him watching the wheels of the tractor. So don't be disappointed if what you thought was fascinating does not feature for your grandchild.

SUMMARY Developing creativity through curiosity, visualization and imagination is very important for the educational environment in which your young grandchild will participate. There is nothing trivial about any of the suggestions in this chapter — these skills set them up for life.

Most of the suggestions cost very little but require patience, understanding and time. These are things that parents sometimes believe they are short of, but it is a perfect role for grandparents to take on. I regularly meet the grandmother of my neighbour's children and she has a PhD in developing creativity. She can be dressed in unusual outfits because she has been told she is a ... whatever. She will sit for ages under a tree helping her grandson hunt for something, she reads the same story over and over, she sings the same requested song over and over, and she helps her grandson find solutions to the plethora of questions fired her way. Her patience is admirable and I love witnessing the gift she is giving her grandchildren. So if you have to 'shop in character' don't worry what anyone else thinks, you are growing your grandchild's creative brain in the best way possible. This stage does not last long but it has a very lasting effect. Enjoy.

9

GIFT GIVING: WHAT TO GET, WHEN AND WHY

I suspect many readers will turn straight to this chapter. I have lost count of the times friends have asked me, 'What is the best developmental gift for my child/grandchild?' There's so much choice and it's hard to separate out the marketing hype from the gifts that are appropriate for your grandchild's stage of development, so this chapter aims to point you in the right direction. Importantly, though, what your grandbaby or grandchild needs most in the world, above all things material, is you and your love.

Grandparents sometimes want to help their children with larger purchases such as a pram, car seat or bike. Make sure you consult with the parents before you commit to large items. They may have specific requirements as to features of the item, preferred styles or colour. Make your offer and then give them options as to how the purchasing is completed.

For smaller items, if you are going to purchase your little one that special gift, it's important to spend some time thinking about the type of toy with which you want your grandchild to play, and the purpose for which it will be used. Aside from price, you need to carefully consider a number of issues:

- Toys need to be geared to the child's age level and developmental skills and to have long-term play appeal. Ask these questions: Will this toy help in any areas of developmental growth? Does it challenge my grandchild's ingenuity?
- Poor quality toys that break easily or break down cause nothing but heartache. Ask these questions: Is this toy safe for my grandchild to use? Is this toy durable?
- Some battery-operated toys and dolls have limited play value, although they have instant appeal, particularly if built up by advertisements. Ask this question: Can the toy be used in different ways? Will my grandchild find this toy interesting a week after receiving it?
- Good quality toys last a long time. Ask this question: Can this toy be passed from one grandchild in the family to another?
- Good toys offer new challenges at different ages. Ask this question: As my grandchild grows will this toy provide a new set of challenges?
- Toys need to be safe. Ask these questions: Does the toy meet approved safety requirements? Does the toy have any little pieces that might come off and be a choking hazard? Will the toy be easy to clean?

All developmental toys should be regularly cleaned. They should also be checked for damage or defects. Any toys that are showing cracks or broken pieces should be replaced. Most developmental toys are designed to be sturdy in order to survive a grandbaby and grandtoddler's rough play, but breakages can still occur.

What to buy before your grandchild is born, or soon after birth

Grandparents often like to help with 'major' purchases of items of furniture that tend to be costly, such as a chair, pram or cot. Many of these can, if they are in a clean and safe condition, be borrowed, handed down, bartered for, recycled or sometimes made.

A gliding or rocking chair

Gliding and rocking chairs are excellent for your grandbaby's development. They are not only relaxing when feeding or reading to the baby, they also provide many opportunities to stimulate your grandbaby's vestibular system. The gentle rocking motion encourages the development of muscle tone, balance and vision. Ideally, every new mother and baby should have access to one of these.

A pram

It's developmentally brilliant to have a pram that allows your grandbaby to lie flat. This provides the baby with the unique opportunity to ride around in the pram on their tummy while awake. This position provides so many more visual experiences and is excellent for muscle tone development and strengthening. This is also wonderful for bonding, communication and speech development.

If purchasing a pram, apart from size, price, colour and practicality there are important developmental considerations to take into account. A few tips on what to look for in a pram (from a development viewpoint):

- The part of the pram on which your grandbaby lies must be completely flat (nearly flat is not okay). It can still be adjustable, so once your grandbaby is sitting up and has the parachute reflex to the side (around eight months), the base can be easily adjusted to a sloping position. Being able to adjust down for sleeping, even for an older baby, is best. Babies who sleep sitting up have been found to risk reducing oxygen supply to the brain, so lying flat is not only best developmentally, it is also a lot safer.
- The pram must have plenty of room for the lying baby to wiggle, stretch arms and legs and roll their body from side to side.
- Your grandbaby ideally needs to be facing the person pushing. Babies who can see their caregiver while in the pram are much happier and calmer.

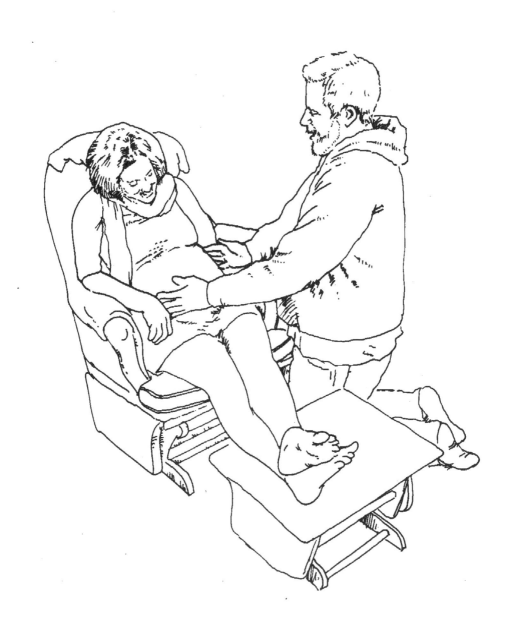

Cots and portable cots

The most important aspect of a cot, or portable cot, is its ability for babies to sleep safely on their backs to reduce the incidence of Sudden Infant Death Syndrome (SIDS). There are strict safety requirements in regard to the gaps between the side bars, height of the railing and space between the mattress and the cot itself. Bumpers, pillows and other additional soft items are no longer considered safe. While the cot frame itself can be secondhand (so long as it complies with the safety rules), do not reuse an old mattress. Old mattresses have been found to contain a toxic bacterium which increases the chance of SIDS. A new mattress should be taken out of its plastic wrapper and aired before a washable mattress protector and fitted sheet is put on. Mattresses are chemically loaded with fire retardants, mould inhibitors and waterproofing agents and airing helps to reduce the immediate chemical insult on the baby.

A bassinet

These are not essential, but many parents like to have the baby in their bedroom, close at hand. Developmentally, the best bassinets swing, rock or sway. Not only does this help sleep, but just like a rocking chair, it stimulates the baby's vestibular system, vision and hearing and calms the emotional system. Bassinets need to be safe and sturdy enough not to tip over. Make sure the mattress is firm and there are no gaps between the mattress and the sides.

Baby capsule for the car

These are certainly the safest way to transport baby when driving. Capsules are, however, ideally left in the car. They are bulky, heavy and totally unsuitable for babies to sleep in at any other time. Not only are they unable to stretch out or move, babies have reduced oxygen intake due to the curled position. Taking them in and out of the car also potentially risks back injury to the adult doing the moving. If you are helping lift your grandchild from the car, take only your grandbaby out, even if asleep, and leave the capsule in the car.

Gifts for newborn babies

Newborns developmentally need love, food and a safe environment in which to sleep. When they are awake, they need the freedom to wriggle and squirm, on their tummies, unrestricted by wraps and swaddling. While gifts for a baby are not immediately necessary, grandparents usually feel the need to give one, and babies do grow and develop very quickly, so here are some suggestions for the first few months.

A playmat

First on the list is the essential playmat. These are fantastic for your grand-baby's development until they are moving. Playmats provide a great way to keep the baby entertained and interested while on their tummy wherever they may be. They encourage the development of big and small muscles, visual skills, hand–eye coordination, foot–eye coordination and more. Try to find one with interchangeable toys that can be easily clipped on and off. You might also find a variety of safe and visually interesting items around the home to attach to the playmat.

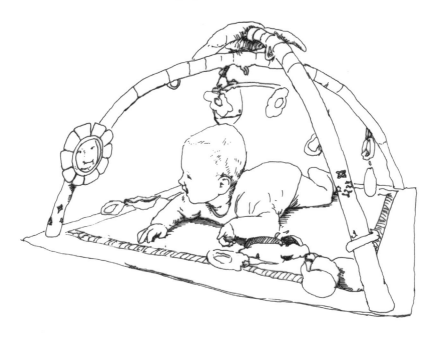

Mobiles

Babies are fascinated by mobiles. While a baby's sight is very limited in distance at birth (to about 15–30 centimetres (6–12 in) — happily the distance between the breast and mother's face) it develops rapidly over the first few months. Your grandbaby will notice contrasts, such as black and white, as well as shadows and flickering light. Mobiles provide excellent visual stimulation, with their movement and shadows, and aid in the development of depth perception and the ability to judge distances. When purchasing a mobile, look at it from underneath so you can see it from your grandbaby's point of view. Some are designed to be attractive from the adult view, but are boring from the baby's perspective.

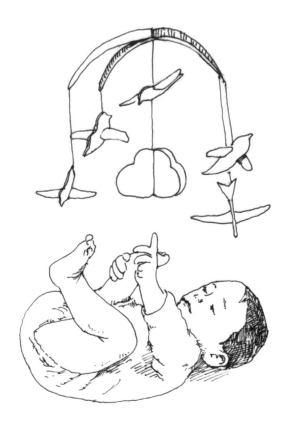

Initial mobile objects can be black and white, to delineate sharp contrasts, and of different shapes, but after a month or two replace these with bright colours such as red, yellow or orange. Babies can distinguish these from other colours by the end of the first month, with blues and purples taking a little more time. While it is thought that babies can see colour from birth, their brain does not yet have the connections to distinguish them clearly. Bright colours enable a contrast between the mobile and the ceiling as they look up.

Because babies get excited by mobiles, they also stimulate movement. Hang them so the bottom of the mobile objects are about 30 centimetres (12 in) from their head at first and then gradually extend the distance to 45 centimetres (18 in) to encourage reaching, swiping and kicking. As your grandbaby reaches out with hands and feet, gross and fine motor skills are being developed along with hand–eye and foot–eye coordination. Find or make a mobile that allows the dangling toys to be changed so your grandbaby doesn't get bored.

Toys

Toys for your grandbaby need to stimulate the development of visual skills, hand–eye coordination, fine and gross motor development and tactile/touch and oral stimulation. Soft, pliable (non-furry) toys that enable a baby to grasp, grab, squeeze and chew them are ideal. The very small baby will enjoy hearing a rattle and feeling and sucking on soft rubber or plastic toys. Toys should be brightly coloured (like the mobiles) and provide a strong contrast, so the baby can easily see outlines and shapes.

While the best objects for babies to look at this age are other people's faces, board books with simple, two-dimensional, flat black and white images are also great. As colour vision matures between four and eight weeks, introduce simple, brightly coloured, two-dimensional picture board books.

Music

Providing your grandbaby with opportunities to hear nursery rhymes and lullabies is important for speech and language development as well as for settling. New parents often do not have a nursery rhyme resource, so purchasing a selection of downloads or CDs is a terrific way to get them thinking about music. Make sure the music is slowed, and simply constructed for children. Babies are learning about the beat of music, so a good beat is important. (Read more in Chapter 7 on music.)

Clothing made from natural fibres

When it comes to clothing, natural fibres are better. Cotton and wool allow your grandbaby's skin to breathe. Fabrics that stretch and allow for lively, natural movement of your grandbaby's arms and legs are also beneficial. Bare feet are best for development so when safely possible, your grandbaby's feet are best kept free of coverings. It is possible to purchase 'grow suits' that do not have in-built feet covers, or look for ones that allow the 'sock end' to be turned back to expose the baby's feet when awake.

Gifts for older grandbabies (5–11 months)

Older grandbabies enjoy exploring a variety of toys that have different sounds, textures, colours and tastes. At this age everything goes in the mouth for the taste test! Hollow blocks or boxes, soft toys, floating bath animals, spinning tops, rattles, squeaky play animals with no removable parts, light plastic blocks, large holed posting boxes, large soft balls and empty containers are all interesting to your mobile grandbaby.

Baby swing

This is my top pick for grandbabies who are sitting themselves up, at around 8 to 10 months of age. A baby swing is a fun way to stimulate the vestibular system, vision, muscle tone and core strength. Prior to this age, all you need to use is your own body. Holding your grandbaby in your arms you can sway, swing, rock and swish around. If your grandbaby is too heavy for you, jiggling, rocking and swaying while lying or sitting baby on your knee works just as well.

Music

It's hard to overstate the importance of music as part of your grandbaby's experience in the first years of life. Music and rhythm stimulate countless areas of development and help prepare the brain for language, timing and movement. Variety and enjoyment are the key here; however, have some music that is rhythmical and has a simple beat.

A pair of maracas

This is the ideal first musical instrument for your grandbaby. As maracas make a sound when moved, they are wonderful for helping to develop auditory and visual skills. Your grandbaby will also learn to reach out for the maracas and shake them by him or herself, as they have a narrow end that they can easily hold. Maracas promote gross motor, fine motor, hand development, hand–eye coordination, thinking skills and more. You can use maracas to help your grandbaby develop a great sense of rhythm and beat — so important for speech and mathematics later in life.

Balls, bubbles and balloons
Your grandbaby will love balls, bubbles and balloons of all shapes and sizes. They are a cheap and wonderful way to encourage many areas of development and learning, including your grandbaby's developing visual skills. They are fabulous for tummy time, muscle strengthening and primitive reflex integration as your grandbaby lifts and moves their head to follow the movement, or chases them once crawling or creeping.

A big-beaded necklace
These are wonderful for mums to wear during breastfeeding. Not only do they help restless, distracted babies during feeds, they are also wonderful for the fine motor development of your grandbaby's hands and the development of visual skills. They need to be sturdy and made from safe materials, so check labels carefully.

Books, books, books
Reading to your grandbaby is such a relaxing and enjoyable activity to undertake. Reading stimulates your grandbaby's speech development, hearing, communication skills and visual development. For your grandbaby's visual development, it is best if books have pictures of a single object with a bold outline. Simple, two-dimensional, sturdy picture books are perfect. My favourite author for this age group is Dick Bruna. It's hard to go past his clear, simple images and short, interesting and often funny stories.

Gifts to avoid
Avoid any broken toys, toys with small removable parts and toys not certified safe by your government safety authority. Please also avoid any kind of screen or 'baby activity' that involves the use of a screen. Baby 'toys' that are

pale, non-descript colours might look cute to an adult but fade into insignificance when viewed by a baby. If they cannot see the sharp contrasting lines, they cannot see it.

There are three items I would particularly like to draw your attention to and urge you not to purchase these as they are developmentally disadvantageous.

WALKERS

There are *no clear developmental benefits* from using a baby walker. Not only are there major safety concerns, research has found that those who use a baby walker are slower to crawl, stand and walk than children who are left to naturally develop these skills. A baby walker also greatly increases a baby's risk of injury from falling, burns, poisoning and drowning.[1]

The problem with baby walkers is that a baby can move around without carrying their own body weight. The muscles and bones of the upper body, back, tummy and legs do not gain strength in the normal way and this, in turn, affects posture and balance. The nervous system is deprived of essential sensory information required for good coordination and body control. These skills are normally acquired through crawling, creeping and cruising. As a result, babies are unlikely to inhibit all the primitive reflexes of infancy or develop strong postural reflexes. This has long-term, ongoing implications for both physical development *and* thinking ability. Interestingly, research has found that babies who had been in walkers did not perform as well in simple mental tasks.[2]

JOLLY JUMPERS

Jolly jumpers are basically in the same category as walkers. These bouncing seats suspend the baby above the ground and encourage them to spring up and down by kicking off from the floor. They take the baby away from the foundational skills of crawling and cruising and are neurological and physically detrimental in the long term.

'BUMBOS' OR ANY BABY SEATS TO HOLD NON-SITTING BABIES IN A
SITTING POSITION

Sitting a baby before they can do it by themselves could interfere with the natural progression of motor skills, each of which plays an important role in later learning and development. Sitting early generally results in less tummy time and this means fewer movement and strengthening experiences, and less opportunity to develop important reflexes that allow your grandbaby to crawl and sit safely and maintain a strong upright posture without falling and banging their head. Babies who are sat up too early are more likely to shuffle along on their bottom. Bottom shuffling is not one of the healthy developmental movement patterns and indicates that the baby still has early primitive reflexes impacting development and movement.

The normal sequence of baby development follows this order: rolling, pivoting, pushing backwards and lurching forward, turning in a circle on their tummy, leading to tummy crawling then crawling on all fours. It is at approximately the same time that babies get into the crawling position on hands and knees that they will push themselves back to sit. So, developmentally, babies don't need to sit until they are just about to crawl on all fours at around eight to ten months.

Being able to sit upright usually occurs after muscle strength in a baby's legs, arms, shoulders and back is well developed through tummy crawling and the brain has matured to a point where important postural reflexes that aid in the healthy development of balance, posture, movement and stability are present.

Gifts for toddlers under two

Before eighteen months, your grandchild does not really need any costly toys at all. Christmas wrapping paper that is shiny and crinkly is probably far more exciting to your creeper/crawler than anything inside! Early walkers will probably prefer the pots and pans in the kitchen cupboards, or the plastic containers from the bottom drawer. Cardboard cartons can be used as cars, fire trucks, buses or trains. If you do consider it necessary to buy your grandbaby and grandtoddler toys, remember they learn through movement and their senses, so the toys and materials for this age should appeal to the senses and the muscles.

As your grandbaby begins to walk they should have simply constructed materials because they experiment continually. A variety of toys is desirable but offer only a few at a time. Rotate toys on offer, so your newly toddling grandchild sees 'new' toys each time they come. Suggestions for your grandtoddler under two years of age include the following.

Scoot-alongs

This is my top pick for the youngest of toddlers. While not quite ready developmentally at their first birthday, scoot-alongs become possible to ride at around fourteen to eighteen months of age. These are pedal-free push cars/toys that toddlers sit on and push with both feet in unison, so they are propelled forward. These aid the maturation of the bilateral development — both sides of the body doing the same job at the same time — and help the brain mature for the next level of skill, jumping (around two years of age). They also help later, more complex skills that enable each side of the body to do different actions at the same time, such as riding a tricycle (one leg is up while the other pushes down), at around two-and-a-half to three years of age.

Toys that can be pushed and pulled

Once toddlers are walking, toys that can be pushed and pulled are excellent for assisting in the development of balance and muscle strength. If the object they are pushing is too light they are likely to fall over more easily. Place some heavy items inside (like two household building bricks) to help your toddler maintain control over the toy. Pull-along, push-along toys are very popular if they make a noise! Large push-along wagons or trucks, in which they can place different toys and objects, are also fun.

Swing set with climbing frame, slide and ladder

By the time your grandtoddler is walking they will also be climbing and

hanging. They love ladders, swings, slides and bars to hang from, so to protect bathroom rails from being broken, a swing set that has the capacity for your grandtoddler to hang from would certainly be a welcome gift. Of course, space is the immediate imperative here. If your grandtoddler lives in an apartment or house with no backyard, you can purchase separate, lightweight trapeze bars, ladders, swings and slides that can be put away at the end of the day.

Musical instruments

Percussion instruments such as drums, bells and shakers are easy to use with both hands and, combined with some music, these make great gifts and help your grandtoddler start to learn about beat and rhythm.

A plastic 'shell'

These can be used for either water play or as a sandpit. Add a bucket and spade; different sized containers that float, sieve or pour water; or some boats (these can also be used in a bathtub).

Objects that replicate real life

This age group loves to replicate and be active participants in day-to-day events. A toy telephone (a smartphone or hands-free are the preferred ones these days); miniature garden tools, household tools like brooms, mops or vacuum cleaners; push-along lawn mowers; and baby doll and a pram are all popular.

Fine motor skill toys

Hand and finger control is still developing accuracy and children of this age need objects that are easy to manipulate and hold: playdough (purchased or homemade — see the recipe below); chunky crayons or chunky chalk and large sheets of drawing paper; soft play animals that can be squeezed and make noises.

Stacking blocks are very popular as they love to build high towers and then knock them over. This is also the time to start a Duplo collection. It

can often be purchased second-hand, and is a gift to which you can easily add. Supply a big box as blocks accumulate over time! There are also great drawstring mats that can be easily made or purchased and which make 'pack away time' painless. Duplo can be used even when children are older, as the large blocks make great garages and sheds in which to store Lego planes or vehicles. This is a gift that will last. The Duplo purchased for my children nearly 40 years ago is now being enjoyed by my grandchildren — in the same drawstring mat!

Books

These need to be very sturdy for this age. Board books with feely pages and lift-the-flap are ideal and engage your grandtoddler in activities as you read the story. These can contain more detailed pictures than those for young babies, but their attention spans are short and so a few words per page is sufficient. *Spot* books by Eric Hill are very popular in this age group.

Indoor toys that stimulate gross motor skills

Some ideas include a crawl-through tunnel (although this can be made from a row of chairs and a blanket); small and large soft balls for kicking, throwing, catching and chasing; hammering sets (which use the muscles of the upper body, arm and hand); a small rocking horse.

HOW TO MAKE YOUR OWN PLAYDOUGH

Playdough is one of the best mediums for hand and finger development and, as your grandchild gets older, for developing their imagination and creativity. Your young grandchild loves putting things in their mouth and given the escalating number of children with food intolerances, here are two recipes in which you can guarantee the contents are safe — one for wheat-free playdough, the other for those who can tolerate wheat.

Wheat-flour playdough	Wheat-free playdough
Ingredients: 1 cup flour 1 cup water 1/2 cup cooking salt 1 tbsp cooking oil 1 tbsp cream of tartar food colouring	Ingredients: 1 cup rice flour 1 cup corn flour 2 cups hot water 1 cup salt 4 tsp cream of tartar 2 tsp vegetable oil food colouring
Method: Mix all ingredients in a saucepan over a low heat until combined well and a dough-like consistency is reached. Remove from the saucepan and allow the mixture to cool. Divide the dough evenly into as many colours as you'd like to make. Add food colouring to each ball until it is just the colour your grandchild is looking for. Store in an airtight container or resealable bag to extend the dough's play life.	Method: Mix the flours, water, salt and cream of tartar in a saucepan over medium heat until thick. Allow the mixture to cool and then add the oil. Knead well over a floured cutting board or similar. Divide the dough evenly into as many colours as you'd like to make. Add food colouring to each ball until it is just the colour your grandchild is looking for.

Gifts to avoid

- As children of this age still often apply the 'taste test' to objects, avoid anything with small parts that may detach or be 'posted' into various bodily openings (like the nose).
- Avoid books with complex pictures and too many words to read. Your grandtoddler has a concentration span of about one to two minutes, but they love books and love turning the pages and lifting the flaps for you.
- Avoid any gifts that involve screen time. Children less than two years of age learn far more from moving and interacting with the world around them.
- Avoid cheap plastic toys that are not sturdy and made to last. In the hands of this age group they will just not last to the end of the day!

Gifts for two-year-olds

Two-year-olds are active explorers of their world. They are learning new things about themselves and their world every day. They are still refining large muscle control, so toys for this age group need to be sturdy and stimulating. Swing sets that include slides, ladders and trapeze bars or monkey bars are very much utilized at this age. They are still only able to developmentally manage scoot-along bikes, although towards the end of this year tricycles and wheeled scooters will become manageable. They still enjoy push and pull toys. Their attention span increases to four to six minutes so they are more able to focus on tasks such as threading beads and stacking toys.

Blackboards and chunky chalk

At the top of the list for two year olds (and up) are blackboards. The bigger and more upright the better! Children use wide arm strokes when initially practising drawing (that's why walls are so popular). Blackboards and chalk are still considered one of the best drawing aids for children. They feel the texture of the chalk across the board and this sends great messages to the brain about touch and movement. They not only get the pleasure of seeing their art on the wall, but they use both their big and small muscles to create their masterpiece. This is especially important for our little ones under six as they still need to learn to control the big muscles of their shoulders and arms so they can then finetune the small muscles of their hands and fingers in readiness for writing at school. 'Chunky' chalk is great for the under-four hands — the chalk is easy to hold and manipulate, and does not break easily. Buy the chalk and a duster from any big store.

While you can buy blackboards, they tend to be far too small for this age group. Blackboards are easy to make. While you can paint walls, kitchen cupboards or back of doors with blackboard paint, it is probably preferable to make one on a board that can be fixed to a wall or held firmly in place and taken down when no longer required. You can make one for your place and one for your grandchild's home. It is preferable to place the blackboard inside the home, in an area where you and the grandchild will most often be. If you place the blackboard in an out-of-the-way place you can guarantee it won't be used! Your grandchild likes to play close to where you are.

HOW TO MAKE A BLACKBOARD

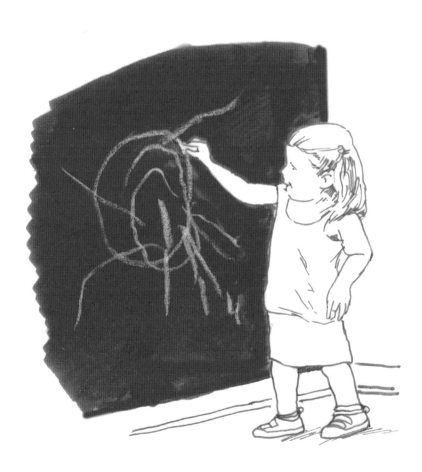

- Obtain a piece of masonite (or similar) 2 metres x 1 metre (2 x 1 yd) if there is space, or smaller if necessary. It should be wide enough for your grandchild when their arms are fully stretched at each side of their body.
- Before you put it up, paint the smooth side with two coats of white sealer paint, lightly sand, then paint with two coats of blackboard paint. When completely dry 'chalk it in'. To do this you need a piece of white chalk and, using it on its side, completely rub it all over the board, then with a duster clean the board. *Note that the blackboard will not work if it is not chalked in first.*
- Mount the board so that the middle of the board is approximately level with your grandchild's chin. If it is a big board, this will mean mounting it at floor level. You can screw or glue the board to the wall.
- Make a grooved wooden ledge to go along the bottom to hold the chalk and stop the chalk dust going on the floor. Don't mount the board over carpet unless you have a plastic strip about 30 centimeres (12 in) wide underneath to catch the dust.

Additional suitable toys for a two year old that enable them to be physically active and to refine balance, develop gross motor skills such as hopping and to develop smaller muscle control by using tools in a variety of ways while exploring and working out how they work are listed below.

Sandpit and water play

Children in this age group are increasingly imaginative and enjoy the sensations they feel through playing with water or sand. It is hard, however, to play without mess, so an outdoor spot, be it in a garden or on a verandah, is required. Buckets, spades and toys that tip, pour, dig, pound and 'make' are all great for sand and water play.

Fine motor skill toys

Fingers are becoming more adept at manipulation tasks, so success in threading, placing and posting is now more often achieved: wooden inlay puzzles (of four to seven pieces), large coloured beads, shape sorters, stacking toys, chunky brushes and non-toxic water-soluble painting materials are all wonderful — although finger and hand painting is very popular in this age group! Playdough and clay for modelling is also great.

Musical instruments and music

Bells, rhythm sticks, shakers, drums, a glockenspiel or a musical box as well as music downloads, CDs or DVDs that encourage them to move and dance.

Gifts for three to five year olds

These children are developing fine muscle control while large muscles are continuing to grow. Their imagination is also blossoming and they love pretend play — to hold tea parties or be tigers in the jungle, firemen, Mummy or Daddy. They continue to love swings, slides and climbing equipment, water and sand play and being outdoors. This age group has a longer attention span and can intensively focus on a task for around twelve to fifteen minutes. They love to work things out and experiment, and often like to

start collecting 'things' they find on walks or in the garden. They very much enjoy their new-found skill of cutting with scissors and pasting with glue. Typically, they talk a lot!

Gross motor skills

My top pick for this age group is a three-wheeled scooter for three year olds, moving to a two-wheeled scooter at four years of age (as balance and motor control refines). Tricycles are also great for three-year-olds, and by four a child can move to a two-wheeled bicycle with training wheels, which should come off by the time they are five if they are given plenty of time to practise. Ball games are also popular — children's footballs (or any kind), plastic golf clubs and balls; a bouncing horse, rocking horse, simple rolling games; a wagon (large enough to hold another child or many items) to push and pull.

Fine motor skills

Help develop fine motor skills with simple throwing games such as skittles; a paddle with ball attached; blunt-ended scissors; paste, hammer, nails and soft wood; a beanbag and target, bubble sets; train sets; 'road mats' and cars.

Thinking games

Matching picture games; a viewer box with slides; magnifying glass; puzzles that have nine to twelve pieces; memory games such as simple 'concentration'; simple construction kits.

Imagination and creativity

Fuel their imagination and creativity with a model house with a small family; farm and zoo sets; a tea party set; washable, unbreakable dolls with a selection of clothes; house-keeping equipment such as brooms, dusters and mops; puppets; simple construction kits; a magnifying glass. A costume box for 'dressing up' can include hats such as space helmets and a firefighter's hat.

Trampolines

Trampolines deserve a special mention. They are fantastic for developing balance, coordination and muscle strength and tone, along with stimulating nearly every sense and every muscle in the body, and they sure are great for fitness. They are in fact, one of the best pieces of sports equipment you can buy for overall development. However, they are only safe if supervised by adults, only one child jumps at a time, and they are dug into the ground or have safety netting. The safety netting removes the opportunity to develop good body awareness in space (i.e. where are the edges and how do I stay in the middle?) but accidents from trampolines over the years mean that netting is now almost mandatory in trampolines purchased for use at home. You can still buy small, lower to the ground trampolines for little ones without netting, or you can purchase a rebound trampoline and remove every second spring (otherwise they are too tight for children to jump on). Again, children need full supervision. If this is not possible, then cross a trampoline off your gift list. Remember to check with the parents first as this is a large ticket item and there may be specific requirements.

Books

Picture books for this age group can be more detailed, both in words and pictures, than for toddlers and there are *so* many great ones it's a just a matter of choosing what you feel your grandchild would like. If your grandchild loves books and reading, then the library really is the best place to find books. Children this age also love stickers and sticker books and simple puzzle books that ask them to find matching pictures or 'hidden' items etc.

Instead of buying a book, a great gift is taking the time to help your grandchild make their own books.

CREATING YOUR OWN BOOK

Creating their own book really gets your grandchild's creative juices flowing, while you have fun together cutting, pasting and storytelling. Any activity can provide a focus for the subject of the book: after an excursion, perhaps to the beach, zoo, museum or visiting friends.

MATERIALS

- Scrap paper, scrap book, computer paper or butcher's paper.
- Scissors, paste or tape.
- Glossy magazines and photographs from any and every source – especially any spare family photos.

MAKING THE BOOK

Fold the paper in half into the size required and either staple or string the pages together at the fold.

Glue the pictures into the book, letting your grandchild choose which pictures to include. Opposite each picture, label the drawing or photo with about three to four words in large print of about 4 centimetres (1½ in). Repeat this on subsequent pages so you have an interesting book that draws together the experience enjoyed by you and your grandchild.

Having books of their own about things they have experienced or seen is a great way to encourage children to love books, introduces them to the printed word and helps them relate to the world around them.

Gifts to avoid

Avoid screens or any screen-based gifts such as subscriptions. Having said that, there are some games and videos that encourage young children to sing and dance or be active. For children in rural areas, there may be online music or sensory-motor classes. An example can be found at www.gymbaroo.com.au where there are online music and movement classes you could purchase for your grandbaby.

SUMMARY Walking down the aisle of a toy shop can be overwhelming. There are simply so many potential gifts for your grandchild. Understanding your grandchild's level of developmental skill is helpful to know before you start looking, and hopefully the suggestions in this chapter have given you some idea of the most appropriate gifts for various ages. Please remember that this list is just a guide and that children develop at their own rate. Some children will be ready for certain activities before others. One grandchild may be three years old, for example, and not quite ready for a tricycle, whereas another may be developmentally able to ride one at two-and-a-half years. If you are in doubt about what your grandchild is developmentally ready for, or you live far away from them and don't know what toys the child already has, then a chat with their parents will go a long way to assisting your choice. It is always advisable to keep the receipt in case the gift needs to be exchanged.

FURTHER READING

Boynton, H. and Brackett. M. 2014, *The Heal Your Gut Cookbook: Nutrient-dense recipes for intestinal health using GAPS diet,* White River Junction Vermont: Chelsea Green Publishing Company.

Goddard Blythe, S. 2011, *The Genius of Natural Childhood*, Stroud, Hawthorn Press.

Jenkins, L. 2012, *Best Start: Understanding your baby's emotional needs to create the best beginnings*, Wollombi: Exisle Publishing.

Porter, L. 2016, *Young Children's Behaviour: Guidance approaches for early childhood educators*, 4th ed., Sydney: Allen & Unwin.

Royal Prince Alfred Hospital. 2019, *The Diagnostic Elimination Diet Handbook Volume 1*, Sydney: Royal Prince Alfred Hospital.

Sassé, M. 2002, *Tomorrow's Children: For parents*, Melbourne: Toddler Kindy Gymbaroo.

Sassé, M. 2009, *Smart Start: How exercise can transform your child's life*, Wollombi: Exisle Publishing.

Swain, A.R., Soutter, V.L., Loblay, R.H. and The Royal Prince Alfred Hospital Allergy Unit, 2019, *Friendly Food: The essential guide to managing food allergies and intolerances*, Sydney: Murdoch Books.

Endnotes

Introduction

1   Ee, N., Maccora, J., Hosking, D. and McCallum, J. 2020, *Australian Grandparents Care: A companion report,* Canberra: National Seniors Australia.

2.   Statistics New Zealand 2017, 'Grandparents lend a hand for childcare', www.stats.govt.nz/news/grandparents-lend-a-hand-for-childcare.

3.   Zhang, J. Emery, T. and Dykstra, P. 2020, 'Grandparenthood in China and Western Europe: An analysis of CHARLS and SHARE', *Advances in Life Course Research*, 45, https://doi.org/10.1016/j.alcr.2018.11.003

4.   Age UK press release, '"Grannannying" is the word as five million grandparents take on childcare responsibilities', 17 September 2017.

Chapter 1

1.   Shonkoff, J.P. and Phillips, D.A. 2000, *From Neurons to Neighbourhoods: The science of early childhood development,* 2nd ed., Washington DC: National Academy Press.

2.   Mustard, J. Fraser 2010, 'Early brain development and human development', *Encyclopedia on Early Childhood Development*, www.child encyclopedia.com/pages/PDF/MustardANGxp.pdf.

3.   National Scientific Council on the Developing Child 2018, 'Understanding Motivation: Building the brain architecture that supports learning, health, and community participation: working paper no. 14', www.developingchild.harvard.edu

4.   Levitt, P. 2007, Presentation to the US House of Representatives, Panel on the Science of Early Childhood Development, National Summit on America's Children, Washington DC.

5.   Meaney, M. 2010, 'Epigenetics and the biological definition of gene x environment interactions', *Child Development*, 81(1), pp. 41–79; National Scientific Council on the Developing Child 2010, 'Early experiences can alter gene expression and affect long-term development: working paper no. 10', www.developingchild.net

6.   Perry, B. 2000, 'Principles of neurodevelopment: An overview', A Child Trauma Academy Presentation Series 1, No. 2, www.ChildTrauma.org

7.   Tau, G.Z. and Peterson, B.B. 2010, 'Normal development of brain circuits', *Neuropsychopharmacology*, 35(1), pp. 147–68.

8. National Scientific Council on the Developing Child, 2018.

9. National Scientific Council on the Developing Child, 2018.

10. Fox, S.E., Levitt, P. and Nelson, C.A. 2010, 'How the timing and quality of early experiences influence the development of brain architecture', *Child Development*, 81(1), pp. 28–40.

11. Knudsen, E. 2004, 'Sensitive periods in the development of the brain and behaviour', *Journal of Cognitive Neuroscience*, 16(14), pp. 12–25.

12. Kolb, B. and Whishaw, I.Q. 2015, *Fundamentals of Human Neuropsychology*, 5th ed., New York: Worth Publishers.

13. Doidge, N. 2007, *The Brain That Changes Itself: Stories of personal triumph from the frontiers of brain science*, New York: Penguin.

14. Knudsen, 2004; Chen, C-H. et al. 2012, 'Hierarchical genetic organization of human cortical surface area', *Science*, 335(6076), pp. 1634–6.

15. Kandell, E.R., Schwartz, J.H., Jessell, T.M., Siegelbaum, S.A. and Hudspeth, A.J. 2012, *Principles of Neural Science*, 5th ed., Connecticut: Appleton & Lange.

16. De Giorgio, A., Kuvacic, G., Milic, M. and Padulo, J. 2018, 'The brain and movement: How physical activity affects the brain', *Montenegrin Journal of Sports Science & Medicine*, 7(2), 63–8, doi: 10.26773/mjssm.180910; Grohs, M.N., Reynolds, J.E., Dewey, D. and Level, C. 2018, 'Corpus Callosum microstructure is associated with motor function in preschool children', *NeuroImage*, 183(2018), pp. 828–35; Diamond, A. 2007, 'Interrelated and interdependent', *Developmental Science*, 10(1), pp. 152–8; Diamond, A. 2013, 'Executive functions', *Annual Review of Psychology*, 64, pp. 135–68; Grossberg, S. 2012, *Studies of Mind and Brain: Neural principles of learning, perception, development, cognition, and motor control*, Boston: Springer Science and Business Media.

17. von Hoftsten, C. 2004, 'An action perspective on motor development', *TRENDS in Cognitive Sciences*, 8(6), pp. 266–72.

18. Wolpert, D. 2014, 'The real reasons for brains', TEDGlobal, www.ted.com/talks/daniel_wolpert_the_real_reason_for_brains.

19. Grossberg, S. 2012.

20. Schwartz, A.B. 2016, 'How the brain communicates with the world', *Cell*, 164(6), pp. 1122–35.

21. Hannaford, C. 1995, *Smart Moves: Why learning is not all in your head*, Virginia: Great Ocean Publishers.

22. Koziol, L.F. and Lutz, J.T. 2013, 'From movement to thought: The development of executive function', *Applied Neuropsychology: Child*, 2(2), doi:10.1080/21622965.2013.748386; von Hoftsten, C. 2009, 'Action, the foundation for cognitive development', *Scandinavian Journal of Psychology*, 50(2009), pp. 617–23, https://doi.org/10.1111/j.1467-9450.2009.00780.x

23. Diamond, A. 2000, 'Close correlation of motor development and cognitive development and of the cerebellum and prefrontal cortex', *Child Development*, 71(1), pp. 44–56; Diamond, A. 2007; Thelen, E. 2004, 'The central role of action in typical and atypical

development', *Movement and Action in Learning and Development: Clinical implications for pervasive developmental orders*, edited by I. Stockman, pp. 49–73, Amsterdam: Elsevier Academic Press.

24. Williams, J. 2015, 'Does a neurodevelopmental movement program affect Australian school children's academic performance? Unlocking Potential: A report', *Australian Journal of Child and Family Nursing*, 12(2), pp. 12–18.

Chapter 2

1. Common Sense Media 2017, 'The Common Sense Census: Media used by kids age zero to eight', www.commonsense.org/research.

2. Piaget, J. 1936, *Origins of Intelligence in the Child,* London: Routledge & Kegan Paul.

3. Thelen, E. 2004.

4. Bangsbo, J. et al. 2016, 'The Copenhagen Consensus Conference: Children, youth and physical activity in schools and during leisure time', *British Journal of Sports Medicine*, doi: 10.1136/njsports-2016-096325.

5. Getman, G. 2000, *How to Develop Your Child's Intelligence*, Los Angeles: Optometric Extension Program Foundation Inc.

6. Thelen, E. 2004.

7. Perry, B. 2000.

8. Goswami, U. 2015, *Children's Cognitive Development and Learning*, York: Cambridge Primary Review Trust.

9. Prechtl, H.F.R. 2007, 'General movement assessment as a method of developmental neurology: New paradigms and their consequences', *Developmental Medicine & Child Neurology*, 43(12), pp 836–42.

10. Blomberg, H. 2011, *Movements That Heal: Rhythmic movement training and primitive reflex integration*, East Melbourne: Beyond the Sea Squirt.

11. von Hofsten, C. 2004; Grossberg, S. 2012.

12. Blomberg, H. 2011.

13. Melillo, R., Leisman, G., Mualem, R. and Ornai, A. 2018, 'Persistent childhood primitive reflex reduction effects on cognitive, sensorimotor and academic performance in school-aged children with ADHD', *Frontiers in Public Health*; Goddard Blythe, S. 2018, *Movement: Your child's first language*, Stroud: Hawthorn Press.

14. Melillo, R. et al. 2018; Goddard Blythe, S. 2018.

15. Kretch, K.S., Franchak, J.M. and Adolph, K.E. 2014, 'Crawling and walking infants see the world differently', *Child Development*, 85(4), pp. 1503–18.

16. Goddard Blythe, S. 2018.

17. Hansen, K., Joshi, H. and Dex, S. 2010, *Children of the 21st century (volume 2): The first five years*, London: The Policy Press.

18. Piek, J.P., Dawson, L., Smith, L.N. and Gasson, N. 2008, 'The role of early fine and gross motor development on later motor and cognitive ability', *Human Movement Science*, 27(5), pp. 668–81.

19. Berthoz, A. 1997, *The Brain's Sense of Movement* (trans. Giselle Weiss), Cambridge, MA:

Harvard University Press.

20. Alloway, RG., Packiam Alloway, T., Magyari, PM. and Floyd, S. 2016, 'An exploratory study investigating the effects of barefoot running on working memory', *Perceptual and Motor Skills*, doi:10.1177/0031512516640391.

21. Leisman, G. 2018, '"I" and "Thou": Cognitive-motor interaction in the development of individuation', presentation at the Movement and Cognition conference, Harvard University Medical School.

22. Source of finger plays: www.preschooleducation.com/sland.shtml.

Chapter 3

1. Salzwedel, A.P., Stephens, R.L., Goldman, B.D., Lin, W., Gilmore, J.H. and Gao, W. 2018, 'Development of amygdala functional connectivity during infancy and its relationship with 4-year behavioral outcomes', *Biological Psychiatry: Cognitive Neuroscience and Neuroimaging*, doi: 10.1016/j.bpsc.2018.08.010.

2. National Scientific Council on the Developing Child 2004, 'Children's emotional development is built into the architecture of their brains: working paper no. 2', www.developingchild.net.

3. Moya, F. 2018, 'Emotion and education: How they work together', INPP conference presentation, Madrid, Spain.

4. Bauer, J. 2014, 'Basal neurobiological systems behind the psychological development of children: Motivation, stress, mirror neurons and aggression', INPP conference presentation, Vienna, Austria.

5. Meaney, M. 2010.

6. Bauer, J. 2014.

7. Lovic, D. 2010, 'Stress in mind, body and brain', INPP conference presentation, Vienna, Austria.

8. Cline, F.W. and Fay, J. 2006, *Parenting with Love and Logic: Teaching children responsibility*, 2nd ed., Colorado Springs: Nav Press.

9. Moffitt, T.E., Poulton, R. and Caspi, A. 2013, 'Lifelong impact of early self-control', *Scientific American,* 101, pp. 352–9.

10. De Giorgio, A. et al. 2018.

11. Bauer, J. 2014; Chakrabarti, L., Scafidi, J.V. Gallo, V. and Haydar, T.F. 2011, 'Environmental enrichment rescues postnatal neurogenesis defect in male and female Ts65Dn mouse model of Down Syndrome', *Developmental Neuroscience*, 32(3), pp. 249–56.

12. Lovic, D. 2010.

13. Lupien, S.J., McEwen, B.S., Gunnar, M.R. and Heim, C. 2009, 'Effects of stress throughout the lifespan on the brain, behaviour and cognition', *Nature Reviews Neuroscience*, 10, pp. 434–45.

14. Mast, F.W., Preuss, N., Hartmann, M. and Grabherr, L. 2014, 'Spatial cognition, body representation and affective processes: The role of vestibular information beyond ocular

reflexes and control of posture', *Frontiers in Integrative Neuroscience*, doi.org/10.3389/fnint.2014.00044.

15. Mast, F.W. et al. 2014.

16. Berthoz, A. 2000, *The Brain's Sense of Movement*, Cambridge, MA: Harvard University Press.

17. Ayres, A. J. 2005, *Sensory Integration and the Child*, Los Angeles: Western Psychological Services.

18. National Scientific Council on the Developing Child 2018.

19. Meaney, M. 2010.

20. Bauer, J. 2014.

21. Bauer, J. 2014.

22. Masten, A.S. 2013, 'Global perspectives on resilience in children', *Child Development*, 85(1), pp. 6–20.

23. Rutter, M. 1987, 'Psychosocial resilience and protective mechanisms', *American Journal of Orthopsychiatry*, 57, pp. 316–31. doi:10.1111/j.1939-0025.1987.tb03541.x.

24. Masten, A.S. 2013.

25. Kidd, S. 2010, 'Resilience in homeless youth: The key role of self-esteem', *American Journal of Orthopsychiatry*, 78(2), pp. 163–72; Ekeland, E., Heian, F. and Hagen, K.B. 2005, 'Can exercise improve self-esteem in children and young people? A systematic review of randomised controlled trials', *British Journal of Sports Medicine*, 39(11) http://dx.doi.org/10.1136/bjsm.2004.017707.

26. Campbell-McBride, N. 2010, *Gut and Psychology Syndrome: Natural treatment for autism, dyspraxia, A.D.D., dyslexia, A.D.H.D., depression, schizophrenia*, London, UK: Medinform Publishing.

Chapter 4

1. Campbell-McBride, N. 2010.

2. Endesfelder, D. 2014, 'The role of gut microbiome in early childhood', Presentation at the INPP International conference, Barcelona, Spain.

3. Endesfelder, D. 2014.

4. Endesfelder, D. 2014.

5. Campbell-McBride, N. 2018, 'Children's health in the modern world', INPP conference presentation, Madrid, Spain.

6. Campbell-McBride, N. 2018.

7. Mitselou, N., Hallberg, J., Stephansson, O., Almqvist, C., Melen, E. and Ludvigsson, J.F. 2018, 'Cesarean delivery, preterm birth, and risk of food allergy: Nationwide Swedish cohort study of more than 1 million children', *Journal of Allergy and Clinical Immunology*, 142(5), pp.1510-1514e.2. DOI: https://doi.org/10.1016/j.jaci.2018.06.044.

8. Krajmalnik-Brown, R., Lozupone,C., Kang, D-W. and Adams, J.B. 2015, 'Gut bacteria in children with autism spectrum disorders: Challenges and promise of studying how a complex community influences a complex disease', *Microbial Ecology in Health and*

Disease, 26:1, doi: 10.3402/mehd.v26.26914.

9. Bergamo, P. 2009, 'Nutrition, neurology and attentive alert angels', *First Steps*, 63, Melbourne: Toddler Kindy GymbaROO; Dengate, S. 2008, *Fed Up: Understanding how food affects your child and what you can do about it*, Sydney: Penguin Random House.

10. Campbell-McBride, N. 2010, 2018.

11. Campos, M. 2017, 'Leaky gut: What it is and what does it mean for you?' Harvard Health Publishing, Harvard Medical School, www.health.harvard.edu/blog/leaky-gut-what-is-it-and-what-does-it-mean-for-you-2017092212451.

12. Bergamo, P. 2009.

13. Vogt, R., Bennett, D., Cassady, D., Frost, J., Ritz, B. and Hertz-Picciotto, I. 2012, 'Cancer and non-cancer effects from food contaminant exposures for children and adults in California: A risk assessment', *Environmental Health*, 11(83), doi: 10.1186/1476-069X-11-83.

14. Trasande, L., Shaffer, R.M., Sathyanarayana, S. and Council on Environmental Health 2018, 'Food additives and child health', American Academy of Pediatrics, Policy Statement. *Pediatrics*, 142(2), e20181408, doi: https://doi.org/10.1542/peds.2018-1408.

15. Lichtensteiger, W. 2015, 'Hormonal active chemicals, brain development and behaviour: What do we know?' Presentation at the INPP International conference, Vienna, Austria.

16. Dengate, S. 2019, Food Intolerance Network Factsheet, www.fedup.com.au/factsheets/support-factsheets/introduction-to-food-intolerance.

17. Trasande, L. et al. 2018.

18. Campbell-McBride, N. 2010, 2018.

19. Yang, T., Doherty, J., Zhao, B., Kinchla, A.J., Clark, J.M. and He, L. 2017, 'Effectiveness of commercial and homemade washing agents in removing pesticide residues on and in apples', *Journal of Agricultural Food Chemistry*, (65)44, pp. 9744–52, https://doi.org/10.1021/acs.jafc.7b03118.

Chapter 5

1. Walker, M. 2017, *Why We Sleep: Unlocking the power of sleep and dreams*, London: Penguin Random House.

2. Xie, L. et al. 2013, 'Sleep drives metabolic clearance from the adult brain', *Science*, 342(6156), pp. 373–7; Fultz, N.E. et al. 2019, 'Coupled electrophysiological, hemodynamic, and cerebrospinal fluid oscillations in human sleep', *Science*, 366(654), pp. 628–31.

3. Smithson, L. et al. 2018, 'Shorter sleep duration is associated with reduced cognitive development at two years of age', *Sleep Medicine*, 48, pp. 131–9; Scharf, R. J., Demmer, R. T., Silver, E.J. and Stein, R.E.K. 2013, 'Night time sleep duration and externalizing behaviors of preschool children', *Journal of Developmental and Behavioral Pediatrics*, 34(6), pp. 384–91.

4. Hupbach, A., Gómez, R.L., Bootzin, R.R. and Nadel, L. 2009, 'Nap-dependent learning in infants', *Developmental Science*, 12(6), pp. 1007–12, doi:10.1111/j.1467-7687.2009.00837.x.

5. Kurdziel, L., Duclos, K. and Spencer, R.M. 2013, 'Sleep spindles in midday naps enhance learning in preschool children', *Proceedings of the National Academy of Sciences of the United States of America*, 110(43), pp. 17267–72, *doi*:10.1073/pnas.1306418110.

6. Walker, M. 2017.

7. Foster, R. 2013, TED talk, 'Inside the sleeping brain', http://inside-the-brain.com/2013/08/20/inside-the-sleeping-brain/.

8. Walker, M. 2017.

9. Talamini, L. 2018, 'The hidden processing potential of the sleeping brain', INPP conference presentation, Madrid, Spain.

10. Smithson, L. et al. 2018; Talamini, L. 2018; Kelly, Y., Kelly, J. and Sacker, A. 2013, 'A time for bed: Associations with cognitive performance in 7-year-old children: A longitudinal population-based study', *Journal of Epidemiology and Community Health*, 67(11), doi:10.1136/jech-2012-202024.

11. Graven, S.N. and Browne, J.V. 2008, 'Sensory development in the fetus, neonate, and infant: Introduction and overview', *Newborn and Infant Nursing Review*, 8(4), pp. 169–72.

12. Walker, M. 2017.

13. Walker, M. 2017.

14. Walker, M. 2017.

15. Pennestri, M.H., Laganiere, C., Bouvette-Turcot, A.A., Pokhvisneva, I., Steiner, M., Meaney, M.J., Gaudreau, H. and Mavan Research Team 2018, 'Uninterrupted infant sleep, development, and maternal mood', *Pediatrics*, 142(6), https://dx-doi-org.elibrary.jcu.edu.au/10.1542/peds.

16. Tonkin, L., Vogel, S.A., Bennet, L. and Gumm, A.J. 2006, 'Apparently life threatening events in infant car safety seats', *BMJ*, 333(1205), doi: https://doi.org/10.1136/bmj.39021.657083.47.

17. Gerard, C.M., Harris, K.A. and Thach, B.T. 2002, 'Spontaneous arousals in supine infants while swaddled and unswaddled during rapid eye movement and quiet sleep', *Pediatrics*, 110(6), e70, doi: https://doi.org/10.1542/peds.110.6.e70.

18. Mitselou, N. et al. 2018.

19. Walker, M. 2017.

20. Scharf, R.J. et al. 2013.

21. Smithson, L. et al. 2018.

22. Smithson, L. et al. 2018; Kelly, Y. et al. 2013.

23. Walker, M. 2017.

24. Scharf, R.J. et al. 2013.

25. Kelly, Y. et al.. 2013.

26. Walker, M. 2017.

27. Goddard Blythe, S. 2014, *The Well-balanced Child*, 2nd ed., Stroud: Hawthorn Press.

28. Walker, M. 2017.

29. Beidel, D.C. and Alfano, C.A. 2011, *Child Anxiety Disorders: A guide to research and*

treatment, 2nd ed., New York: Routledge.

30. Song, C., Zhao, T., Song, Z. and Liu, Y. 2020, 'Effects of phased sleeping thermal environment regulation on human thermal comfort and sleep quality', *Building and Environment*, https://doi.org/10.1016/j.buildenv.2020.107108.

31. Goddard, S. 2005, *Reflexes, Learning and Behaviour: A window into a child's mind*, Oregon: Fern Ridge Press.

32. Loprinzi, P.D. and Cardinal B.J. 2011, 'Association between objectively-measured physical activity and sleep', *Mental Health and Physical Activity*, 4(2), pp. 65–9.

33. Chang, E. and Merzenich, M.M. 2003, 'Environmental noise retards auditory cortical development', *Science*, 300(568), pp. 498–502.

Chapter 6

1. Smith, A. 2006, 'Speech motor development: Integrating muscles, movements and linguistic units', *Journal of Communication Disorders*, 39(5), pp. 331–49, doi.org/10.1016/j.jcomdis.2006.06.017.

2. Leisman, G., Moustafa, A.A. and Shafir, T. 2016, 'Thinking, walking and talking: Integrative motor and cognitive brain function', *Frontiers in Public Health*, 4(94), doi: 10.3389/fpubh.2016.00094.

3. Shonkoff, J.P. and Phillips, D.A. 2000.

4. Johnson, J.S. and Newport, E.L. 1989, 'Critical period effects in second language learning: The influence of maturational state of English as a second language', *Cognitive Psychology*, 21(10), pp 60–99.

5. Kuhl, P. 2010, 'Brain mechanisms in early language acquisition', *Neuron*, 5(9), pp. 713–27.

6. Kuhl, P. 2011, 'Early language learning and literacy: Neuroscience implications for education', *Mind, Brain and Education*, 5(3), pp. 128–42.

7. Hutton, J.S., Horowitz-Kraus, T., Mendelsohn, A.L., DeWitt, T., Holland, S.K. and the C-MIND Authorship Consortium 2015, 'Home reading environment and brain activation in preschool children listening to stories', *Pediatrics*, 136(3), pp. 466–78, doi: https://doi.org/10.1542/peds.2015-0359.

8. Sosa, A.V. 2016, 'Association of the type of toy used during play with the quantity and quality of parent-infant communication', *JAMA Pediatrics*, 170(2), pp. 132–7.

9. Radesky, J.S., Schumacher, J. and Zuckerman, B. 2015, 'Mobile and interactive media use by young children: The good, the bad, and the unknown', *Pediatrics*, 135(1), pp. 1–3, doi: https://doi.org/10.1542/peds.2014-2251.

10. Molina, V.J.G. 2017, 'Single vision lenses with additional near-power: Meeting the visual challenge of the digital age', *International Review of Ophthalmic Optics*, www.pointsdevue.com/article/single-vision-lenses-additional-near-power-meeting-visual-challenge-digital-age.

11. Magalhães, L. and Goldstein, J. 2017, *Toys and Communication*, Springer Professional, London, UK: Palgrave Macmillan.

Chapter 7

1. Misuraca, R., Miceli, S. and Teuscher, U. 2017, 'Three effective ways to nurture our brain: Physical activity, healthy nutrition, and music: A review', *European Psychologist*, 22(2), pp. 101–120.

2. Misuraca, R. et al. 2017.

3. Schellenberg, E.G. 2005, 'Music and cognitive abilities', *Current Directions in Psychological Science*, 14(6), pp. 317–20.

4. Rauscher, F.H. and Hinton, S.C. 2006, 'The Mozart effect: Music listening is not music instruction', *Educational Psychologist*, 41(4), pp. 233–8.

5. Fitzpatrick, K.R. 2006, 'The effect of instrumental music participation and socioeconomic status on Ohio fourth-, sixth-, and ninth-grade proficiency test performance', *Journal of Research in Music Education*, 54(1), pp. 73–84; Moreno, S., Friesen, D. and Bialystok, E. 2011, 'Effect of music training on promoting preliteracy skills: Preliminary causal evidence', *Music Perception: An interdisciplinary journal*, 29(2), pp. 165–72.

6. Lazarev, M. 1991, *Sonatal: A program of musical stimulation*, Roseville Services, New York: Bloomsbury; Lazarev, M. 2010, *Mamababy: Birth before birth*, CreateSpace Independent Publishing Platform.

7. Tomatis, A. 2004, *The Ear and the Voice*, trans. R. Prada, P. Sollier, F. Keeping, Maryland: Scarecrow Press.

8. Chang, H-C., Chen-Hsiang, Y., Chen, S-Y. and Chen, C-H. 2015, 'The effect of music listening on psychosocial stress and maternal-fetal attachment during pregnancy', *Complementary Therapies in Medicine*, 23(4), pp. 509–15.

9. Goddard Blythe, S. 2012, *The Genius of Natural Childhood*, Stroud: Hawthorn Press.

10. Warby, S. 1997, 'With love in my heart and a twinkle in my ear', Sydney: Sheila Warby Developmental Education for Suzuki Talent Education Association of Australia (NSW).

Chapter 8

1. Leggett, N. 2017, 'Early childhood creativity: Challenging educators in their role to intentionally develop creative thinking in children', *Early Childhood Education Journal*, 45(6), pp. 845–53.

2. Stehlik, T. 2019, *Waldorf Schools and the History of Steiner Education: An international view of 100 years*, London, UK: Palgrave Macmillan.

3. Gopnik, A. 2010, 'How babies think', *Scientific American*, 303(1), pp. 76–81.

4. Leisman, G. et al. 2016.

6. Fjørtoft, I. 2001, 'The natural environment as a playground for children: The impact of outdoor play activities in pre-primary school children', *Early Childhood Education Journal*, 29(2), pp. 111–17; Swarbrick, N., Eastwood, G. and Tutton, K. 2004, 'Self-esteem and successful interaction as part of the forest school project', *Support for Learning*, 19(3), pp. 142–6.

7. Swarbrick, N. et al. 2004; Bassett, D.R., John, D., Conger, S.A., Fitzhugh, E.C. and Coe, D.P. 2015, 'Trends in physical activity and sedentary behaviors of United States youth',

Journal of Physical Activity & Health, 12(8), pp. 1102–111.

8. Smith, M. et al. 2018, 'Results from New Zealand's 2018 report card on physical activity for children and youth', *Journal of Physical Activity & Health*, 15, pp. S390–92; Leech, R.M., McNaughton, S.A. and Timperio, A. 2015, 'Clustering of diet, physical activity and sedentary behaviour among Australian children: Cross-sectional and longitudinal associations with overweight and obesity', *International Journal of Obesity*, 39(7), pp. 1079–85.

9. Kellert, S. 2005, *Building for life: Designing and understanding the human-nature connection*, Washintgon DC: Island Press.

10. Dankiw, K.A., Tsiros, M.D., Baldock, K.L. and Kumar, S. 2020, 'The impacts of unstructured nature play on health in early childhood development: A systematic review', *PLos One*, 15(2), pp. 1–22.

Chapter 9

1. Schecter, R., Das, P. and Milanaik, R. 2019, 'Are baby walker warnings coming too late?: Recommendations and rationale for anticipatory guidance at earlier well-child visits', *Global Pediatric Health*, 6. doi 10.1177/2333794X19876849; *Australian Competition and Consumer Commission 2019*, 'Product Safety Australia: Babywalkers', www.productsafety.gov.au/products/babies-kids/kids-equipment/baby-walkers.

2. Siegel, A.C. and Burton R.V. 1999, 'Effects of baby walkers on motor and mental development in human infants', *Journal of Developmental & Behavioral Pediatrics*, 20, pp. 355–61.

INDEX